*This book is dedicated to Mum and Dad for starting the obsession with West Ham United and Marie, Melissa and Martin for putting up with me while the obsession grew.*

# West Ham, United Us

1. The Die is Cast
2. Shape of Things to Come?
3. It's A Big Step
4. Home and Away
5. My Favourite Game
6. Home Alone
7. A Difficult Decision
8. Happy Days
9. I Should Be So Lucky
10. Over Land and Sea
11. I've Been Here Before
12. More Regular Than Albran
13. We'll Be Back
14. I've Met My Match
15. Those Are the Breaks
16. Back in the Old Routine
17. Thanks Trev
18. It's Goodnight From Me
19. Moving On
20. Claret and Blues
21. Win Some, Win Some More
22. Premium Bonds
23. Martin Makes His Debut
24. Too Close For Comfort
25. It Must Be Love
26. How Did That Happen
27. Good Friends Are Like the Stars
28. Playing Escalator Football
29. We're All in A Spin
30. A Change is as Good as A Mess
31. Bolton in Disguise
32. Last of the Summer Wine
33. Injury Time
34. Mixed Emotions
35. Extra Time

# The Die is Cast

It has been well documented that we all have one book in us. You have just begun to read my offering. It will make the yellow pages seem like a booker prize winner.

I have followed the Irons all my life through posh and becks, (thick and thin) and not for one moment has it been dull. Apart from the Cup Finals and promotions, West Ham has given me so much more. Through our love of the Hammers, it has been my good fortune to gain the friendship of Steve, Trevor, Dave and Ian. That's something I will always be grateful for and treasure forever.

It's the 25th of May 1954 and I have just collected my first item of West Ham memorabilia, although to be honest I didn't know it at the time. The day is my birthday and the item in question was my birth certificate. Printed on it in large letters are, 'Registration District West Ham, Sub District West Ham Central, and County Borough of West Ham'. I cherish that and am so proud to support my local team, a fact which is all too rare in this day and age. So Mum and Dad left Howards Road Hospital with their Junior Hammer and returned to Corporation Street in Plaistow. I was a caesarean birth but it hasn't affected my way of life, except that is every time I get out of a car I have to go through the sun roof. (Just kidding)

We shared a house with my Dad's sister Rene, her husband John and my cousin Jennifer. It was quite commonplace in those days for two families to share a house. One family would live upstairs while the other took the downstairs.

My Mum, Doreen, was one of eleven and my Dad, Charlie, was one of seven. Times were hard in those days; families especially large ones would often have to do without. Sometimes I would wonder because my parents had seen and lived through such difficulties, was that the reason I was an only child. Not that it ever bothered me because I had many good friends and also it made for a very close relationship with my dad. As life progressed we would watch the Hammers together, work together, holiday together and when he decided to manage a Sunday League football team, I played for him.

I was approaching the age of five when a friend of mum's informed her of a scheme taking place in a new town called Basildon. This entailed working in a local company for three weeks and after that you could get a form from the local corporation to apply for a house. On the form you were able to choose which estate you wanted to live on, how many bedrooms you required and if you wanted a large garden. After returning the completed form, three weeks had passed by and a house was offered. Rent and rates were inclusive and for £2.4s.2d. We had a new home which Mum still lives in today.

Having plenty of family in the East End meant that frequent visits were the order of the day. But, it wasn't till I reached the age of eight that I entered the 'Promised Land' to see the hallowed turf, where in future years I would experience so many mixed emotions. As we all know it's not easy supporting West Ham. You have to be a special type of person because we don't do it for the glory. I was about to fasten my seatbelt for a long and bumpy ride.

# **Shape of Things to Come?**

So with Mum working as a sewing machinist for Christopher Roberts and dad working in the printing trade a new chapter was beginning. As mum and dad's family and friends' 'religion' was claret and blue, it was inevitable that I would be brought into the faith and was just a matter of time as to when dad would decide to take me. That magical day was 3rd November 1962 and we were home to Bolton. My heroes' line-up was Leslie, Bond, Burkett, Peters, Brown, Moore, Brabrook, Woosnam, Byrne, Hurst and Musgrove. A walk to Basildon town centre to get a bus to Laindon station, change at Barking and on to Upton Park. My Dad was concerned that I might not be able to see properly and therefore he had made me a wooden stool to stand on. We were going to stand on the North Bank. About half way back and just to the right is where we were to meet up with the regular crowd, this consisted of my Uncle Tom, Uncle Martin, Uncle Arthur and three of Tom's friends. On arrival there were many youngsters with their home made stools. I can still vividly remember standing in awe when I first saw the pitch and to a young boy the stadium appeared colossal. Outside the ground various stalls would sell many types of souvenirs, I was wearing my bobble hat and scarf Mum had knitted me and I asked Dad if I was allowed any. He agreed and my choice was the claret stars, these had a picture of a player in the middle and you could pin them to your bobble hat, so I chose Musgrove, Woosnam and Moore.

What an eventful game. Lawrie Leslie, the Scottish international goalkeeper, broke his leg in a collision with Bolton's Warwick Rimmer. This was in the days before substitutes were allowed so Martin Peters had to brave it in goal and we played the rest of the game with ten men. Sometimes that's the only way a team can beat the Hammers – if they have a numerical advantage. Bobby Moore never got to score many goals and here on my first visit I got to witness that rare occurrence but, unfortunately, it was in a 2-1 defeat. There was so much to talk about on the way home and I couldn't wait to go again. Even at that age the 'claret and blue spectacles' were beginning to fit perfectly.

Memorial Sports F.C. was the team my Dad played for when we were living in Plaistow, also in that team was his brother Tom and Mum's brother Les. One of mums' other brothers also called Tom, was the manager but obviously with us moving away dad no longer played for them. I can still recall on returning to the East End to visit various family members, time was made to take in a game. They played at the same venue where West Ham (Thames Ironworks as they were called back then) played in their early days. "*Come on the Mems*" was the popular cry from the locals.

Dad and I had many enjoyable visits to Upton Park during the period of 1962-64, we didn't always win (no change there) but the games were always entertaining. In 1963 they played in an American International Tournament and performed really well. The experience would prove invaluable, culminating with the F.A. Cup triumph in 1964. Dad set off with family members to the semi-final in Sheffield with Cousin Martin driving when the heavens decided to open up. The 'liquid sunshine' never stopped all day, (added to the fact that when inside the ground the Hammers fans had been allocated the open end and had to endure a right proper soaking). I've seen footage of the game and if that were today it would've **never** been allowed to start. I think that when Bobby Moore won the toss for kick off he decided to play in the shallow end for the first half.

The team were going to Wembley but only Uncle Arthur was lucky enough to get hold of a ticket. For the Cup Final weekend we were going back to stay with Uncle Tom and watch the game with family and generally 'drink – up' the atmosphere. Canning Town was brilliant for not just the residents, but the retailers were all one hundred percent behind the boys. Many houses were covered in claret and blue, I can recall shops having pictures of the players in their windows. The magazine Charlie Buchan's Football Monthly issued a Cup Final special edition, big colour pictures of the lads from this publication appeared everywhere. People were so happy, filled with excitement and anticipation. My Uncle Les and Aunt Elsie had a flat in Green Street. He invited friends over for the game, created his own programmes and even arranged seating to replicate seating within a stadium. We weren't great in the first half but improved in the second. We were 2-1 down at half time, Johnny Sissons being our goal scorer, and then a header from Geoff Hurst brought us level in the second half. This really lifted the crowd and just to hear 'bubbles' echoing around the stadium gave me goose bumps. It was still two each with just a few minutes to go, I had been desperate for the loo for quite some time and couldn't hold it in any longer. I quickly dashed out and whilst 'splashing my boots' a loud cheer went up. Hurriedly I rushed back in to be greeted by the sight of mad celebrations. We had won the cup with a goal in the last minute – and I had missed it!

Peter Brabrook had crossed from the right and Ronnie Boyce had arrived in the box to head into the far corner of the net. Will someone please hurry up and invent videotape. As we were staying for the weekend, the choice to attend the victory parade was a no brainer. We were by the Abbey Arms pub and it seemed the 'world and his wife' were there. I was perched on Dad's shoulders to watch the coach slowly pass along, en route to the Town Hall. The players were proudly showing off the F. A. Cup, being a West Ham fan is easy, no trouble at all. (Really?)

I'm glad we won as Uncle Les's makeshift 'stadium' didn't get vandalised. I never got to spend much time with him at Upton Park as he loved to be in the Chicken Run. Part of the match day ritual for us was the little games that we played for in – match enjoyment. Bearing in mind dear reader this was in the days when players wore shirts numbered one to eleven. The game would involve a piece of paper being torn into six separate pieces. Written on five pieces would be the number seven, eight, nine, ten and eleven, on the final piece would have the letter D written on it. They would then be folded up and each player selected one. The number drawn by that person related to the West Ham player wearing that shirt number. For example, if you picked nine you'd have Byrne, if it was ten you'd have Hurst etc. If you picked D, that meant you had the whole defence (all players from one to six). Now the game would start and should West Ham score, sorry that should read **when** West Ham scored, if it was your player then everyone else would have to pay you one shilling. So one goal from your player would earn you five – bob, not too shabby back in the day. This also gave an added bit of interest to the game we were watching. Another game played was when only four were involved; each person would choose a corner flag, for example Chicken Run/South Bank, or West Side/South Bank. Whenever a corner was awarded on your quadrant for either team the other three players would have to pay you one shilling. An open palm was the signal given by the player to request payment, if you forgot that was your quadrant and didn't ask then your chance to be rewarded had gone. The final game was played when there were more than six people. One person would begin at kick off holding a marble, or some such similar object. When a corner was awarded to any team on any quadrant, they should pass the object to the next person and at the final whistle whoever was holding that object would have to pay a pre - arranged amount to all the other players. Many a time you would be so engrossed in the game you would often forget to pass it on. Simple, fun games, probably a forerunner to today's betting. Now its first goal scorer, score casts, amount of goals in the game, more or less anything you care to ask for.

I was later to discover we had a celebrity friend of the family; this was the dear departed Alan Sealey. The very same who would go on to score the two goals at Wembley to win the European Cup Winners Cup against TSV Munich. He had picked up my Cousin Martin from school on occasion and I too would get the chance to meet him, I suppose my Uncle Tom was the closest to him. One Saturday we were doing the rounds of visiting and on that evening who should turn up but Alan Sealey. West Ham had been away to Spurs and played out an exciting 4 - 4 draw, Alan then proceeded to talk us through all the main events and was very sociable. There were to be a couple more coincidence meetings with Alan, on one such visit he offered to take my autograph book with him to training. He was as good as his word and did this for me; I still have the autograph book today and is one of my prized possessions. There are some great signatures. Apart from Alan there are Jim Barrett Senior, Bill Lansdowne Senior, Phil

Woosnam, Geoff Hurst, Martin Peters, Iain Crawford and John Lyall just to name a few. The only unfortunate thing on my part is that when Alan took the book into training, Bobby Moore was away on international duty. Uncle Tom kept a scrapbook just on Alan's career alone, from being spotted playing local football via Leyton Orient to breaking his leg after Wembley. I am pretty sure that it is still somewhere in my loft after it was passed on to me. It's a great shame that his career and life were ended way too early. When returning from games Dad would take me to a big sports store called Leach. My first pair of West Ham socks came from that shop (this was a time before club shops and replica shirts were worn at games). Those socks were all white with one claret band and one blue band round the top.

# It's a Big Step

By now I was getting a bit too tall to stand on the wooden stool but not tall enough to stand with the adults and still have a comfortable view. For this reason I moved away from where the family stood to find a vantage point more beneficial to my needs. Instead of entering the North Bank and walking straight ahead you could turn to the left and walk upwards, this would lead to an area affectionately known as 'the cage'. It had steps that were so much bigger, so if a taller person would stand in front of me my view wouldn't be impaired. I tried to make my way to the far side because then I would be as close to the seats in the West Stand Upper Tier as possible. The family knew that was my favoured position and so could keep a watchful eye on me. At first it seemed strange having nobody to talk to during the action. It's amazing really but during the trials and tribulations of the game you make the sounds of 'ooh' and 'ahh', turn to someone and a conversation would soon be struck up. Where I was standing there seemed to be quite a few youngsters with similar ideas regarding viewing positions. There were occasions where 'the cage' would fill early and I was unable to get in. This was a blow as the position was almost like being in the stands; it provided the height even though you had to stand.

The following season produced another fantastic cup run, this time in Europe and most of the family had tickets for the cup final as opposed to last season. I was to discover that lady luck was not on my side. My final year at Kingswood Junior School was approaching; we were called fourth year pupils. It was customary that the fourth year pupils had the opportunity to go on a holiday abroad, which had to be planned months in advance. The parents were given what were called paying in books and whenever they wanted to, the parents could pay as much or as little of the cost. This particular year the trip was to Spain and Portugal, I asked Mum and Dad if I could go and they readily agreed. They had the card and were paying off the money gradually, this was also about the time the Irons were embarking on that magical cup run. When I first asked to go I never imagined the boys would get to the final and, to make it worse for me, it was going to be at Wembley. The inevitable happened, we won the cup and I am out of the country. The holiday was a cruise and at the time of the final we were out to sea; in fact, I think it was two or three days before we saw land. I think that's correct but as the boy in the orthopaedic shoe's said "I stand to be corrected". Trying to get the result was nightmare but eventually we managed to get hold of a newspaper. In the stop press all that was written was the score West Ham 2 TSV Munich 0, there were no pictures no match report about our heroes what a let-down. But at least we had won and would be back in the competition the following year. So I had missed the winning goal in F.A. Cup Final and now all of the Cup Winners Cup Final, right now my luck was so bad that even the Samaritans were hanging up on me! I have one image clearly imprinted in my memory and can still recall it as if it was yesterday. We were arriving home and the ship was about to dock at Tilbury and there were crowds of parents on the quayside waving to their children but I had no trouble picking out my Dad as he was standing there giving me the cross hammers with his arms. Mum and Dad wanted to know about the holiday whereas I wanted to be talked through the game. When I found out that it was Alan that scored both goals that was just the icing on the cake. He would've been on cloud nine unaware that that in the not too distant future his footballing days would be over.

The lads were training at Chadwell Heath and decided to have a game of cricket. Whilst trying to take a catch, Alan ran and tripped over a bench breaking his leg. It was one of those benches that would be used for either sitting or standing on when the team photos were being taken. We had identical ones at our school which were used for P.E. Anyway, Alan eventually recovered and returned to the first team but was never the same player as he was.

After just a handful of games he moved on to Plymouth, then Romford and after experiencing the highs and lows of the professional game he went into business.

My baptism into the West ham fold had been both exciting and entertaining and the good times were set to continue. As holders of that European trophy we defended it with distinction the next year before going out to the eventual winners Borussia Dortmund from Germany in the semi-final. My dad took me to the F.A. cup game when we played Blackburn Rovers and that was another Michael Jackson (thriller). A crowd of over 32,000 saw us draw 3-3, and then we would lose the replay. In the league cup we reached the semi-final and disposed of Cardiff City 10-3 on aggregate. West Bromwich Albion were too strong for us in the final but still a great achievement. A measure of our success that year was the fact that we had played 62 games, and the players of today complain if they have to play twice a week.

In 1966-67 I was part of one of our biggest attendances in years when I was present for the F.A. Cup match with Swindon Town. The figure that day was 37,000 plus. Served up before us was another treat in the shape of a 3-3 draw. This in no small way due to a hat trick from Geoff Hurst. We lost that replay too, it appears we have trouble performing again so quickly (isn't that right lads). At only twelve years of age

West Ham are certainly helping me with my education. They are teaching me new words like giant- killing, shock and upset. In November in four consecutive games we scored twenty goals and beat Fulham, Leeds, Spurs and Newcastle. In December in six consecutive matches we score twenty-one goals including an incredible 5-5 draw with Chelsea in front of nearly 48,000 fans. Entertaining times indeed, how good was my introduction to life at Upton Park. I wasn't going expecting to see us win, that was never an option. But the style of football Ron Greenwood had us playing I was going expecting to see goals. Defeat in the semi-final of the league cup this year would inflict double the amount of pain. This was the year it had been decided to do away with a two legged final and play it at Wembley. West Bromwich Albion are the team about to piss on my cornflakes. If it wasn't for bad luck, I wouldn't have any luck at all.

During those years the lads would never run out to the tune of bubbles, it would be the post horn gallop that would announce to the crowd when our heroes were about to emerge. I would generally look towards the centre of the chicken run as those would be the ones to get the first glimpse being directly opposite the tunnel. Another give away sign would be seeing the small old man (his name was Paddy) in front of the tunnel, gesturing to the crowd with his arms to make some noise. Another character I can recall was Monty; He was dressed in a type of military uniform, marching down Green Street blowing his bugle. He would stand on the South Bank and in between the so called music he would be shouting and hollering. Back in the day vendors could be seen on the terraces peddling their wares. There was the man in the white coat selling peanuts, the type where you had to break the shell to get the nut. Also, even though it would be early afternoon there would be the chap selling the Evening News and the Evening Standard which would carry previews and pictures of the days' matches. Before the times of DJ's, we were entertained by the British Legion Band. The chap on the cymbals seemed to have his own fan club in the West enclosure; they gave a great cheer every time he crashed them together. This was the scene, a friendly relaxed atmosphere with no hint of trouble. Well, it was until Manchester United came to town in 1966-67. They needed to beat us to become champions which they duly did 6-1 (or was that the first set, best of three). Dad took me to the game and for the first time was really concerned for my safety. We were in the main forecourt area awaiting entry into the North Bank. The place was heaving then, all of a sudden, bottles were being flung our way and fights were breaking out all over the place. Dad was wearing a long overcoat and he undid the buttons then pulled me in close and told me to hold around his waist. The coat was then buttoned up again with me inside for protection while he tried to slowly walk with me to the wall at the back, near the turnstiles. Later I found out that this was to ensure no bottles would be coming towards us from the rear and Dad would only have to look in one direction to avoid the missiles. Once inside the ground the fighting continued during the game. It was a scary time and I asked myself "is adrenaline meant to be brown?"

# **Home and Away**

By this time my Dad wasn't going to away games. Even so, he would tell me tales of the games he went to during the championship winning season 1957-58. Travelling there on his Brother Tom's motorbike, he even went to some away games then but it suited him more to just stick to the home games. I was still quite young at the time but he didn't mind me going to away matches providing he knew I was safe. My Dad was working at a printers and one of his work mates was a nice guy called Norman Hyde, well, as nice as it gets for a Spurs supporter. This would be in 1966 and Norman and his son were going to White Hart Lane to see them take on West Ham. Norman and Dad were working overtime the morning of the match and it was suggested by Norman that if I got to the factory as they finished work it would be alright for me to go with them in their car to see the game. Well, I wasn't going to pass up on an opportunity like that and what a great decision by me it turned out to be. It was an electrifying end to end derby in front of a crowd of over 50,000 and they saw us come from behind to lead 3-2 at half time, with goals from Byrne, Brabrook and Sissons. In the second half we rode our luck as Spurs hit the woodwork three times and Jimmy Greaves even missed a penalty, which in itself was about as rare as my mate Steve getting a round in. Spurs then equalised and made it 3-3 and with ten minutes remaining it looks like we will be going home with a point but then, Geoff Hurst grabs the all-important winner. Happy days.

Another stand out memory from that time was to occur the following season. My Cousins husband Brian and his brother Peter both of whom are Chelsea fans (their medication hadn't kicked in yet) were going to Stamford Bridge for the visit of the Hammers. No problems with Mum and Dad and off we go in Peter's car. Brilliant! Another away win, this time 3-1 and all in the world is rosy. Later that season we are drawn away to Burnley in the F.A. cup and win 3-0, that game Burnley were lucky to even get nil. The fourth round draw paired us with Stoke playing at their place.

Now, across the road to me lived Steve Anderton. He was about the same age as me and, like me, was a West Ham fan too. His family were going by car to Stoke; I can't remember the exact model of the car but I know it was an Estate. Behind the back seat there was a space where luggage would be stored, Steve's Dad said if I was prepared to sit in that space I could travel with them. What! My first proper away game outside of London. I said "You can even strap me to the roof rack if it means I get to go". Me and Steve wound down the windows of the car, and then wedged our scarves in them so they would blow in the wind while we were travelling along the road. We also stuck up some pictures of a team photo and Hurst, Moore and Peters on the back window. It was easier to get pictures of those three because of their heroics in the World Cup and their pictures were everywhere to be seen. The journey was great, passing fans would be tooting their horns, waving and giving us the thumbs up, and the cherry on top of this already great day would be that we creamed Stoke 3-0. We even afforded ourselves the luxury of Geoff Hurst missing a penalty; he absolutely smashed it against the bar. I certainly slept well that night dreaming of going to Wembley and the draw for the fifth round did nothing to harm those dreams.

It was a home tie with Sheffield United who we had already beaten in the league 3-0, added to the fact that the Blades were struggling at the foot of the table. Myself and my Dad went together full of confidence but, West Ham being West Ham went and got beat 2-1. This would be good practice for me as I would endure many more occasions such as this. To rub salt in the wound, not long after this we beat them at Bramall Lane in a league match. And yes, they were relegated and we finished safely in mid table. How can you treat me this way West Ham?

# **My Favourite Game**

When going to West Ham with my Dad, not all of our journeys would be by train. Sometimes my Uncle Arthur wanted to drive and we were offered a lift in his van. After the car was parked and we were ready for the walk to the stadium, it wasn't unusual for us to be greeted by a couple of lads who would then offer to 'look after the car' for a small fee. This in itself was a thinly disguised threat that if failing to comply there was a fair chance that your car would get damaged or even possibly stolen. Arthur told us of one such instance when after parking he was approached by two young lads. One of them straight away asked "Look after your car mister, only two bob". Uncle Arthur replied "No thanks boys, there's a dog in the back", and quick as a flash the boy said "Can it put out fires". Now looking back, I reckon that probably wasn't true but nonetheless a story well worth including.

By this time, I had taken on a paper round to earn some extra money. It was an evening round and I was employed directly by the Evening Standard and not by a newsagent. It would be six nights a week, the Monday to Friday wasn't too bad but the Saturday nights were really tough. I had quite a large round during the week but on Saturdays it was almost four times as big. The reason for all the extra customers was simple; we delivered an edition called the Classified. This had all the football results and was packed with reports, pictures and goal scorers; this was to prove so popular with the customers. After I had finished delivering the round on a Saturday I went straight home to work out how many papers I had sold, I needed to do this so I could check to see how much I had earned and if it was enough for the next home game. Steve from across the road also worked for the Evening Standard and as we were growing up we were going to matches together as well as with other mates. A couple of lads who lived on our street would go with us along with one other important person who would go on to play such a big part in my life. This day will always be a pivotal moment in my life, the day we met.

I was attending Kingswood Junior School, and at the time it was sponsored by IKEA (our assemblies took ages). I was a member of the school football team and on this particular day we were playing away at a school called Greenstead. Neither of our sports teachers had a car nor did the school have a mini-bus, so every away game we had no choice but to walk there. Not the most ideal of preparations and there were definitely no overnight stays in a hotel for us, anyway, I digress. After getting changed to play we went out onto the pitch and the Greenstead team were already out there having the pre-match kick about. I then noticed that one lad was wearing a claret tracksuit top with a large West Ham badge on it over his shirt. As I went past him I felt the need to talk to him, I can't remember the exact words I said to him but I think they were along the lines of "I'm a Hammers fan too, have you ever seen them play?" it was a brief exchange of words but the ice had been broken. I could only get the reply yes before we were both called away by our coaches. We won the game 4-1 and both of us had scored for our team. This has got to be my favourite game ever but not because myself or the team had played particularly well but because I had just met Steve Lloyd, who would feature heavily in my life and be a great friend. Several weeks later we were drawn away in the cup and fate had returned us to Greenstead where I was up against Steve again. This time the conversation was a bit longer, I asked him if he was still going to matches. During the conversation he said that him and some friends were going to Saturday morning pictures in Pitsea and asked if I wanted to meet them there, we did this a couple of times. One day Steve mentioned he played football on a Saturday morning for a team called Bela United and asked if I wanted to join them. I jumped at the chance and this would be the first of many teams we would play in together. I had joined a really good team and we went on to win the league and cup that year. With regard to the cup tie between our schools Kingswood came out on top with a

4-0 victory, and we made it all the way to the junior schools cup final. Whitmore School were the current holders of the trophy and would be facing us in the final. Sadly for us they retained their grip on the silverware courtesy of a 2-0 win.

It was now getting towards the end of the sixties and Steve was coming with us to some games at Upton Park with the lads who lived on my street. I took the eleven plus examination, passing the exam would mean going to a Technical Grammar school and failure, I would be off to a Secondary Modern. Well, I didn't pass and so it was Secondary Modern for me. On my school report for Geography it read "Does well to find his way home." History and Maths were my four best subjects. Anyway I was fine with the outcome because Steve would be going to the same school. We both made it into the football team and represented the school from under 12s to under 15s. There is one game I will never forget that I attended with my mates. We were at home to Nottingham Forest in the season of 68-69 and my mates were on the North Bank. Whenever West Ham scored in those days the crowd would surge forward, pushing you nearer the front. Geoff Hurst scored and sure enough we all went running down the steps; however, on this occasion I felt a smack on the top of my head. At the time I just put it down to high spirits and thought no more of it, how wrong I was. It wasn't until later that I realised that somebody had flattened chewing gum into my hair. Try as I might, but I was unable to pull it out, I had to endure an embarrassing journey back home where Mum used scissors to repair the damage. I ended up looking like the chief member of the Friar Tuck Appreciation Society. So now our friendship was well and truly established Steve Lloyd was now going to matches with me and my other friends.

Steve Anderton's family favoured the West Side enclosure so stood with us on the North Bank. One of the first evening games I went to was in the 65-66 season at home to Sunderland. I was at the front, close to the wall and Harry Redknapp sent over a corner and Martin Peters was there to thunder home a header. Being so close to the action was brilliant. I could hear the thud of the ball as Peters met it with his head, and as he turned away to celebrate I could even see the sweat on his face. For the benefit of Benni McCarthy sweat is something that happens when you run around for a bit.

# **Home Alone**

It was around that time my Nan had been unwell, she had taken a turn for the worse and had been admitted to hospital so Mum and Dad had decided to take me out of school. We went to stay at the flat in Green Street with Uncle Les and Aunt Elsie as they lived closer so this meant we could visit her more often and for longer. Well I say we, but in effect it was actually my parents that visited more often. Having a large part of our family still living in the East End meant frequent visiting trips, for me the highlight of these excursions was when we stopped off at East Ham to call in to Cooke's to indulge in their famous pie, mash and liquor. This was one of my favourite meals, a fact that still holds true to this day. Both of my children would grow up to appreciate this east end delicacy but more about them later.

During our short stay, the Hammers had a friendly against Kilmarnock on a Friday night and as it was only a short walk I went along to see us win 2-0. The friendly was part of a deal when we were about to sign their goalkeeper Bobby Ferguson, personally, I was never a great fan of his. I felt he didn't command his penalty area enough and after hearing the Gordon Banks story I would become even more disappointed with the signing. Manager Ron Greenwood was in the market for a new goalkeeper and he decided to make an approach for Gordon Banks, who at the time was England's number one. In a turn of events Greenwood was then told that Banks was not for sale, however, should the situation change that West Ham would be first in line and could have first refusal on him. In the meantime he approached Kilmarnock about bringing Ferguson to us, the answer came back that because they were still playing in Europe they wanted to hang on to him but as soon as they got eliminated he would join us. Greenwood had agreed to this and whilst waiting, Leicester came back to say they were ready to sell Banks and are we interested. Greenwood though, having already given his word to sign Ferguson, had passed up the opportunity to sign him. What a choker that was. We could've had four of England's World Cup winners in our team and with a world class keeper, who knows how our fortunes may have changed. Oh well, it costs nothing to dream.

Sad to say that Nan passed away but it was a comfort to know that she was surrounded by her family.

My first proper evening game that I went to on my own was a League Cup tie against Hull. Steve Anderton, Gary and Kenny were all supposed to be going but for various reasons were unable to go. I wasn't too keen on going to matches on my own but if the only alternative was to miss the game, then I went.

I was now attending senior school and making new friends, like one fellow Hammer called Adrian Goldfeather who was always good company. We were both in the same year but not the same tutor, although we did attend some of the same lessons together. We went to a few home games with each other and the first one would be for the visit of Manchester United. I had my paper round money and Adrian got some cash together. Relating to my previous experience of when Man Utd came we thought that it would be wise to pay the extra cost and have a seat. This way if things did get a bit naughty behind the goal we could watch from the comfort of our seats, which were back then on a first come, first served basis. This type of fixture regularly attracted huge crowds so we knew if we wanted to have half a chance we needed to arrive early. We arrived on the forecourt at about 10.00am with our packed lunches and the turnstiles would not be open for another two hours but thankfully the weather was kind to us. Well, after waiting for what seemed like an eternity we got our seats, unfortunately after all the hype and expectation the game itself was a massive let down and ended in a 0-0 draw. When myself and Adrian left senior school we went our separate ways and were no longer to stay in contact.

With reference to the aforementioned Man Utd fixture, the pricing arrangements for this type of game had always been a pet hate of mine. When the so called 'big guns' visit us e.g. Man City, Man Utd and Chelsea, they are classed as category A games. In accordance with the decision prices are therefore much higher. Why? Do the players get paid more for these games? Can the club guarantee a better class of game? More goals? So why the extra cost. As I have previously explained, I witnessed a very uninteresting 0-0 with Man Utd, which would have been classed as category A. On the other hand, you have the visit of Bradford City in 2000, probably a category C game, produces a 5-4 thriller. The logic for this escapes me.

Arriving really early for a match as described for the Man Utd disappointment was always preferable to getting to the ground and not being able to get in due to being a full house. Fortunately, I was never to endure that particular scenario. Even so, there were a couple of instances where I turned up only to be confronted outside the main gates with a large sign saying Match Off – Pitch Frozen.

Whilst talking about football in general and discussing the merits of other sides, my friend Steven Ryan sought my opinion when he asked me "What do you think of football at White Hart Lane?" I replied "I think it would be a good idea".

At the start of the 70-71 season West Ham would draw five of the first six matches and I managed to be present for four of those. The first would be away to Spurs and on the opening day of the season too. Stephen Ryan and Steve Anderton were to be my travelling companions that day. It was fated that Jimmy Greaves would score for us against his old club; from our vantage point on the shelf we had a great view of his strike after an equally great knockdown from Geoff Hurst. It was an enjoyable game which finished all square 2-2. Another game in the sequence that I witnessed was the home match versus Southampton; this was also a draw and finished 1-1. It does remain in the memory though for one particular reason and that was being one of the best goals I had ever seen at Upton Park. Unfortunately, it was by Tommy Jenkins of Southampton, he was a talented outside left. He ended a long, mazy dribble past five players with a fine finish.

# A Difficult Decision

As much as I loved going to West Ham games by the same token I really enjoyed playing. I was already playing Sunday league football with a side called Long Riding, naturally, Steve Lloyd was also playing for them. We started out in the fourth team at the club and worked our way up to appear in the first eleven. It would prove to be competitive but the better standard of football in the area was played on a Saturday. It was a difficult decision because in those days we didn't have the type of blanket coverage that today's game enjoys. Match of the Day on a Saturday night would only feature two matches while The Big Match on Sunday would feature one game from the London area but not necessarily from the top division. Quite often the cameras would be at the likes of Brentford or Charlton and that's what made my choice a tough one. It is different today because if you support a Premier League side they're going to be shown whatever the outcome, you can play on Saturday knowing you can watch your team that evening. So I would miss a lot of West Ham games, but on the other hand I wouldn't be able to play forever. The enjoyment I got from playing football told me I should make the most of this time and attain the best level possible. After all, there would be mid-week league games, possible home draws in the League Cup,

F.A. Cup replays – there was still a chance to do both.

Mum was brilliant with a pair of knitting needles and she knitted me a jumper in the style of a West Ham Shirt, she also made one for dad to wear so he didn't feel left out. It was the away shirt, sky blue with two claret hoops; it looked really great and was a sad day when I grew too big to fit into it. I remember wearing it to work once and workmates were asking where they could get one.

I was now playing for a team called Pemberry Athletic in the Mid Essex League. You guessed it, with Steve Lloyd again and another good mate Billy Bingham who had also been a team mate in our successful Bela United side. Now it would be a case for waiting for a mid-week game to come along so I could get my 'fix' of claret and blue. During this time, season tickets were as rare as Billy Bonds having a bad game. Steve's Dad had got one for the East Stand Upper Tier and had let me use it for the final home game of the 70-71 season where we would be playing Huddersfield Town. For some unknown reason Steve's Dad was unable to attend and Steve was playing cricket so I was third in line to the throne, as it were, to acquire the ticket. A 1-0 defeat did little to spoil my enjoyment of having a seat with such a spectacular view. This experience told me to get my name on the waiting list for a season ticket, so I applied for it and carried on playing and thought no more of it. My 18th birthday arrived and my parents got me a brilliant present, it was the West Ham rug I had been wanting. This was too good to put on the floor even though the quality was Axminster. If I put it on the floor people would be walking all over my West Ham and I wasn't having any of that. Even though I had seen a few teams do that to them in the past. Instead I had the rug mounted and it took pride of place hanging on my bedroom wall. It's still part of my collection of Hammers memorabilia.

I was working in a factory and Steve Lloyd was working in tailoring but we still kept in touch during the week. He would come to my home for dinner one week and the following week his Mum, also called Doreen, would cook me a meal at their home. Sadly, Doreen and Husband Dave are no longer with us but I shall always have fond memories of them as they made me so welcome in their home. The parties they hosted on New Year's Eve at their home were always wonderful occasions; it was always a pleasure to get my regular invitation.

Still eager to attend whenever possible, we never had a fixture when Spurs were due to play at our place so I was free to go. I was with Gary and Ken who wanted to go in the West Enclose. We took up our position adjacent to the players' tunnel and were within touching distance of the teams as they came out. It was customary then that about one hour or so before kick off the away team would come out onto the pitch still dressed in their suits. They would tend to congregate in the centre circle just generally looking around the stadium, inspecting the pitch and browsing through the programme. So on this particular day as Spurs came out, I was so close that I handed my programme to the Spurs defender Cyril Knowles and asked him if he wouldn't mind signing it. He did this and proceeded to join the rest of the team. Upon returning back down the tunnel I asked Cyril Knowles for his autograph, he obliged and said "You've got my autograph twice now". I responded by saying "Yes, and if I can get it three more times I will have enough to swap them for one of Billy Bonds'". I do now have an autograph from Billy Bonds but on the down side we let Spurs go away with a point after a 2-2 draw.

# **Happy Days**

Before videotapes and DVD's, the most popular way to watch old games was by cine-film. The producers of these tended to go for the more high profile games such as cup finals, major internationals and world cup games. I began to take an interest in this and bought myself a projector, an adjustable table for the projector to stand on and a screen. You will not be surprised to learn that my collection began with the West Ham films that were available. These would be the 1964 Cup Final against Preston North End, the 1975 Cup Final against Fulham and the European Cup Winners Cup Final against TSV Munich. If you wanted them with sound you were charged extra. However, they had one little gem available which I couldn't wait to purchase and view. There was a shop in Romford that would sell these, so I went off eager to buy the production of West Ham 8 Sunderland 0 which had the text 'Six Goal Hurst' on the front cover. This was a real collector's item because Geoff Hurst hit a record six goals in that match. It only lasted for ten minutes but was great viewing. Even the other recordings would only last for about fifteen to twenty minutes because they would just show the main highlights. I did expand the collection beyond West Ham mainly opting for games that produced plenty of goals. Some of these films have now been sold on (except the West Ham ones of course). With new technology being developed it was no surprise that this format would die out but not before I had a night when the lads came round for an evening of cultural entertainment. I do believe that to be the most fit and proper way to describe watching West Ham footage.

Whilst playing on Saturdays and Sunday, I wished for the Irons to have a cup run in order that I might get some more games in, well, I didn't have to wait too long for my wish to be granted (note to self - with that in mind I must wish for a nice win on the lottery). The League Cup provided the ideal opportunity and we played some good stuff in that run including an away win at Leeds, who at that time were always at the top of the league. A home win over Liverpool and a 5-0 thumping of Sheffield United, we owed them that one. These performances led us to Stoke in the Semi-Final, a 2-1 away win in the first leg and I go and get measured up for my suit. Then came the second leg at home and I didn't arrive as early as I intended because I had to work a little bit later. The crowd was huge, almost 39,000 and I didn't want to spend a lot of time fighting my way through them so I just made it to the nearest turnstile and went into the West Enclosure. It was a tense, nervy affair with Stoke scoring near the end to force extra time. In the dying minutes of the game Harry Redknapp was brought down by Stokes' Gordon Banks in the box for a penalty and I'm thinking Wembley here we come. In the first leg Geoff Hurst scored a penalty, hitting it hard and high to the keeper's right. He chose to hit in the same place again only for Banks to guess correctly this time and save it. I think it was Taylor, Bonds and McDowell who didn't look when it was being taken, if only Banks had chosen to do the same.

I never went to the first replay which was being played at Sheffield but I did go to the next one at Old Trafford. Myself and Steve Lloyd both took the day off work and went by coach, it took the best part of six hours. On parking up the driver said "After you've won, you will want to celebrate so I will pick you up one hour after the final whistle". The game was eventful to say the least; Bobby Ferguson got knocked out so Bobby Moore went in goal. Moore then went on to save Bernard's penalty but he netted the rebound. Hurst got lumps kicked out of him all game, sometimes in the box but the referee doesn't award us a penalty. We go 2-1 up only to lose 3-2. It had been pouring down and John McDowell started our downfall with a dodgy back pass that got trapped in the mud. After the final whistle it was still raining and all the pubs are full of celebrating Stoke supporters, while me and Steve are getting soaked waiting for the driver after hanging about for an hour. I get home just before 6am and I had to be at work by 8am. For that reason it wasn't worth going to bed and it was no surprise that I got sent home before lunch as I kept falling asleep. A day that had been typical of my luck, when my ship comes in I'll be at the airport.

Trevor Brooking would go on to form an amazing understanding with Alan Devonshire, but in my opinion the partnership with Pop Robson would run it pretty close. I always felt sorry for Robson because he had a brilliant season plundering 28 league goals and never got a sniff of the England squad. Also, after giving us good service he left the club and missed out on us winning the F.A. Cup. Not long after he would be back at the club, and yes, when he left us for a second time we would go on to win the F.A. Cup again. At this point in the proceedings Steve would introduce me to three of his friends and from that day on they were to become my best friends too. These lads were Trevor Ridley, Dave Craft and Ian Nixon. Steve himself was very knowledgeable on the Hammers, he could play most sports and was better than average at most of them. Trevor was into martial arts and ten-pin bowling, while Ian loved motor racing and would even go to Grand Prix's and the qualifying sessions. Dave didn't tell jokes; he didn't need to because he is just a naturally funny guy with a heart as big as the London Stadium. All these lads are great company and I have never gone home after being in their company and not felt better for the experience.

They say in life you are lucky if you find one good friend, well I have found four.

Brian Carson was a friend of my parents and was one of the good guys and the next event that I relate will perfectly illustrate the point. My uncle Les had been offered a job in Peterborough so he and my aunt Elsie made the decision to leave Upton Park and take up the challenge in pastures new. Once settled we were invited up for a long weekend. The 'we' in question being Brian, mum and dad, me and Steve Lloyd. We left to return home on the Monday afternoon and Brian drove us all back to Basildon. That evening West Ham were at home to Coventry City and Brian suggested if Steve and I wanted to go he would drive us there. So after having something to eat with us he then drove us to the game and dropped us off home afterwards before returning to his home in Aveley. What a star. Brian and his friend Dave Palmer were to become firm friends with all our family, more of which later.

As for the game itself it was our first home game of 1972/73 and we won 1-0 thanks to a hotly disputed header from Clyde Best. Had the whole of the ball crossed the line? All that mattered was that the linesman said yes it had (and no he wasn't Russian).

# I should Be So Lucky

Trevor and Steve worked for the post office and played football for them in the Wednesday league, now and again I would turn out for them if I could get the time off of work. Steve was very versatile and could do a great job at either centre back or centre forward but truth be told, cricket was his game. Trevor was often compared to Billy Bonds; people would say "Compared to Billy Bonds, you're rubbish". Myself and Billy Bingham had left Pemberry where we had ended the season as cup winners and league runners up. The cup final was a wonderful evening played at Billericay Towns' ground. We beat the league champions 3-0 with two goals from yours truly, and one from Billy Bingham. My mum rarely came to see me play, but on that evening she was present with my dad to watch which made the win even more special. So Billy and I are now playing for Chadwell Heath in the Essex Olympian League, meanwhile Steve signed on for another season with Pemberry. Playing for Chadwell Heath was a great opportunity to go to Upton Park providing our game was postponed and the Hammers were at home. Two instances remain fresh in the memory because we really did 'land a touch'. The first was in the 74-75 season and our home game with Collier Row is called off due to the condition of our pitch. Billy Bingham, Paul Pearson, Steve Cunnew and I jumped in a taxi and headed for the Boleyn for the home game against Wolves. To be fair, the Upton Park pitch wasn't much better than ours at Chadwell Heath but Brooking effortlessly glides over the mud to inspire the boys to a thrilling 5-2 victory. My pick of the goals in a five-star performance was a free kick that was cheekily flicked up by Brooking and then Frank Lampard smashed home a beauty. It was great to be able to do that, just turn up and be able to get in. It was so unexpected to be at the match and then get treated to a sublime display, to quote that immortal philosopher "Lovely Jubbly".

The second of the postponements happened about three months later. Our game was called off and this time we were at home to Burnley, good fortune was certainly smiling on me that day. The same group of us went and as always, I bought a programme. Well, West Ham get to the F.A. Cup Final and in the ballot for tickets it's announced that the lucky numbers would come from the programme versus Burnley. I checked my programme and the numbers printed inside were a match. I was going to Wembley, how lucky was that? Where dad worked they knew he was a big fan of the Irons and one guy came up trumps for him. The man in question was a cousin of Kevin Lock and got dad a ticket. But not only that, it was for the same enclosure as mine. We booked our coach tickets with a local company and were now set. I have described how seeing Upton Park for the first time was so special but seeing the claret and blue filling Wembley was something else. Then when the boys wearing claret and blue appeared on the pitch the feeling was sensational. I have no doubt that all of the team had dreamt of playing there, well I had always dreamed of seeing them there. For the neutrals it wasn't by any means a classic but when it's your team you just want it to go your way. Two goals from Alan Taylor saw us beat Fulham 2-0 and qualify for Europe again. I think we had some of the 'falling down water' that night.

Back on the playing front at Chadwell Heath, we had won the league and were about to play our own Cup Final. It would be played at Chelmsford City's ground against Collier Row. Two weeks prior we had played them in the league and beaten them 3-0, however, on this day they took their revenge and reversed the 3-0 score line (so we didn't qualify for Europe). Dad hadn't seen many of the Saturday games that season even though he saw most of the Pemberry games. He was still there on the touchline every Sunday as the matches in those leagues tended to be more local. It was very empty feelings when the season had finished because Steve would play cricket and me and Trevor would regularly meet up and go ten pin bowling on a Saturday morning. They should have put the pins in those little gullies at the side, we would have scored more. Dave Craft was interested in cars, particularly banger racing, something at which he was quite good. He had won races (even though there were times when he had to stop to ask for directions). On the one occasion I went to see him in action at a venue near Tilbury and he never managed to complete the first lap, but undaunted still greeted us with a smile and a laugh when we met up afterwards, I imagined Lewis Hamilton slept easy that night.

# Over Land and Sea

In 1976 Billy and I left Chadwell Heath to play for Bowers United in the Essex Senior League. I graduated from the reserves to the first team and made my debut against Billericay Town. They beat us 3-1 and would go on to win the F.A. Vase, this was no great surprise as they really were a quality side. We were training twice a week and this was the fittest that I had ever been. I couldn't wait for match days to come around. Steve had now joined me and Billy Bingham playing for E.S.L. which was our Sunday league side. Billy and I had just completed one happy season with E.S.L. and finished runners up in the league. Saturday football was more serious than our Sunday side, even though it consisted of mates who were more than useful. Steve, Trevor and I were joined by Derek Entwhistle for our annual holiday; I had wanted to go to the Far East (Great Yarmouth) but got outvoted. The outcome was to be booking a fortnight in Jersey. None of us had ever been before and we were really looking forward to this break. We flew from Southend airport and it was going to be about a one-hour flight. The lady in front of me had never flown before and was terrified. She turned to me and asked, "If I open that door will we fall out?" My reply was "No, I will still talk to you". For first time flyers it must be very un-nerving when you arrive at the airport and the first thing you see is a large sign saying TERMINAL.

Having been told that the best beach on the island of Jersey is at Brelades Bay, we waste no time in paying it a visit. So there we are having a kick-about on the beach when we notice a coach arrive. The guys getting off the coach seemed to be familiar, and sure enough when they got closer we recognised Terry Venables and Kenny Sansom. It was the Crystal Palace football team who were on tour. I had a pleasant chat with Terry Venables who then kindly agreed to have a photo taken with me. He told us where they would be playing their next match should we be interested in going. We watched them train for a while before leaving. Acting on Terry's information we did go to see them play. We left mid-way through the second half as by then Crystal Palace were already 8-0 up, and it wasn't much of a contest. Whilst staying at the hotel we met a lovely family, the Dovey's who came from Worcester. Ken and Lydia had two children about the same age as us. They were called Ian and Kay and Lydia asked if it was possible they could hang out with us. That was no problem for us because they were so down to earth and easy to get along with, so much so that we would stay in touch for almost fourty years. That holiday still holds many fond memories of time spent with such lovely people. After they found out we were West Ham fans they invited us to stay with them if ever we were in their neck of the woods. A trip was planned to go to the league game away at Aston Villa so we decided to take them up on their kind offer. Steve had recently purchased a new Ford Fiesta and therefore was quite happy to do the driving. So Steve, Trevor, Derek and I set off for Villa Park in search of an away win. What a great day. Alvin Martin made his debut, and Trevor Brooking hit a 'cracker' from about twenty-five yards. Well it would have been a great day if we had not cordially invited them to plant four in the back of our net. Having put on our black arm bands we got back to the car and headed off to Malvern in Worcester. It had been arranged that we were going to a restaurant to meet up with the Dovey family. After an enjoyable meal it was back to Lydia and Ken's home where we were made most welcome for the rest of the weekend. Their kindness was greatly appreciated by us all. But that still did not stop us from poking some gentle fun at them. We asked if stage coaches were still delivering the mail round there, and that their village was so small the mayor and the village idiot were probably the same person.

Our quest for European glory was a fantastic journey. I was enjoying my Saturday football with Bowers United but I made sure I never missed any of those wonderful home European ties. Those evenings were really something special, culminating in the most magical of evenings against Eintracht Frankfurt, but looking back I'm surprised the game was ever allowed to go ahead. The pitch was atrocious but the atmosphere was electric, with us fans singing our hearts out. Trailing 2-1 from the first leg this 3-1 victory will live long in the memory. Trevor Brooking never let the quagmire of a pitch hamper yet another stylish, match winning performance and capped a brilliant display with two quality goals. Keith Robson launched a missile into the top corner of the net to send us in to party mode. I'm pleased to say for that every one of those home games my dad was by my side, if I could have picked anyone to share that night with it would have been him. At the final whistle we just hugged each other and then stood staring at the pitch, we didn't want to leave. A night like this seemed a million miles away that evening when I stood on the terraces in Den Haag for the quarter final first leg.

A few people I knew were going but they were going on the day trip, whereas Steve and I made a booking for the three-day trip. We took off from Southend airport armed with our European travel cards. These were in effect 'good boy behaviour cards'. When booking an away trip in this competition this card needed to be produced. Now if you had been on an away trip and had got in to any sort of trouble your card would have been confiscated. Therefore, being unable to produce the card meant no more European travel, thus hopefully encouraging the fans to behave. We arrived at our hotel in Rotterdam and found out it was the hotel where the player's wives are staying. A coach was provided to transport us to the stadium which in my opinion rated as no more than an average championship ground. It made a change for us hammers fans to be in a section along the touchline, and not shoved into a pokey enclosure by a corner flag. As usual the claret and blue army had travelled in numbers. Before the game I witnessed an incident that made me laugh out loud. Let me picture the scene for you. We are walking along the road and about twenty five yards in front of us is a police car pointing away from us. A West Ham fan for reasons unknown was being arrested. The police officer opened the back door and threw him in, almost immediately the door on the other side opened and he jumped out and ran away. Viewing this from behind was hilarious and a big roar went up from the boys in claret and blue.

Back to the game, its half time we are 4-0 down and West Ham are having a Weston. Sorry if I have lost you there, allow me to explain. If you are having a bad game it's often referred to as 'having a mare'. This is taken from the word nightmare. Well if you are having a really bad game a Weston is 'a Super Mare'. Nothing has been going right, we have given away two penalties, their full back has scored a hat-trick, and the ref keeps stopping the game to make our lads pull their socks up! Billy Bonds, Tommy Taylor, Graham Paddon, and Keith Robson quite often would play with their socks rolled down, what is going on here? During half-time, and as the players came out for the second half we were singing "we'll be running round Brussels with the cup" to try and inspire the boys. Did I really believe what I was singing? In all honesty I thought I had more chance of being handcuffed to a ghost. With the fans not giving up on the team it's times such as these that I'm immensely proud to be a hammers supporter. In the second half Billy Jennings scored twice and we get out of that one only 4-2 down. Now do you know what, we've got half a chance here. The lads do the business in the home leg as we turn it around with a 3-1 win to go through on the away goals rule.

When the game in Holland was over Steve and I went back to our hotel and watched the highlights on television before going out on the town. Making our way through the city centre it was impossible not to notice the 'working girls'. One of these girls was the owner of the biggest pair of boobs that I have ever seen. How can I best describe them? I suppose you could say that she looked like a dead heat in a Zeppelin race! We encountered no trouble and I'm glad that we had opted for the three-day trip.

It was good not to have to rush straight back home and having free time to see some of the country.

After the near perfect home performance in the semi-final against Eintracht Frankfurt we are now in the final. Up against us will be the Belgian side Anderlecht and they have the advantage as it's being played in their back yard, the Heysel stadium to be exact. I don't suppose we can complain; after all it was similar for us in 1965 against T.S.V. Munich at Wembley. Getting to the final was the least the team could have done for us and to say our league form was disappointing would be an understatement. From the final twenty one games we only managed one victory. So we travelled with a great deal of optimism as we thought they were saving their best performances for the cup.

Soon after getting match tickets we booked the coach and eagerly awaited the day. Not only would Trevor, Steve, Dave and I be going but also joining us was Sparrer. I only got to know Sparrer via Dave and it is a great shame that he is no longer with us as he passed away all too soon. I had to get up at 5.45am as the coach would be leaving at 7.00am, the thought of an early start did not go down too well with me. I made Rip Van Winkle look like an insomniac! Anyway, we make it on time and the driver heads for Felixstowe, upon arrival we will get the ferry to Zeebrugge then drive to Brussels.

Our driver must have been the original 'Victor Meldrew'. He didn't like us singing, wouldn't let us put the radio on, was reluctant to stop for us and we had stuck pictures of the players on the windows and he immediately told us to take them down. All he kept saying to us was "You'll have to grovel to them, otherwise they'll give you stick". This was reference to the local police and almost instantly the chant 'Grovel and stick' went up. It lasted nearly as long as the famous 'Billy Bonds Claret and Blue Army'. We arrived at the ground two hours prior to the kick off, getting our priorities right we decided to go for a beer and what a lovely pub it was. As we entered there was a long corridor where, towards the rear, crates were stacked up full of lager. Naturally all the Hammers fans assumed this was the local's way of welcoming us into their country. Not wanting to be rude, the claret and blue pilgrims took full advantage of the generously provided refreshments. People were just helping themselves to the drink, taking them outside to break off the bottle tops on the window ledges. After a while Dave, Steve, Trevor and myself chose to move on and we were now in good spirits singing 'Bubbles' for all the locals to appreciate as we walked through the city. We then heard klaxons that were really loud and getting closer to us followed by the noisy chant of 'Anderlecht, Anderlecht, Anderlecht'. From round the corner their fans appeared and there must have been at least thirty of them so we stopped singing and crossed the road. Copying our movement they too crossed the road and made a point of walking towards us, as this happened Trevor began to roll up his sleeves. I turned and asked Trevor what he was doing, I will never forget his response and it was thus "Well if I'm going down, I'm taking a couple of 'em with me". They carried on walking towards us and when the biggest guy was standing right in front of us, he held out his hand and said "West Ham United. Good team. Good luck tonight", shook hands and walked off again. We had to laugh; we thought it was all going to kick off.

So we are going to see the match after all, Steve and myself were the only ones to get a programme that night. It was a big European final but there didn't seem to be many sellers about, how I wish I had kept that programme. Another purchase I made before the game was a stick of rock, it was claret and blue and West Ham was printed throughout. This would be something to show the lads at work when I got back. We have another drink close by the stadium and the kick-off time is approaching. I'm now carrying the flag Dave had brought along, a giant Union Jack with West Ham United in white letters stitched across it. All very well you might think but it's nailed to two pieces of two by four. I'm now thinking they'll never let me in with this but then again what do I know –

straight in to take up my position in the Upton Park choir. I was the third tenor on the left. The game gets underway and we're looking alright then about half an hour passes and Patsy Holland scores. Get clouds seven and eight out of the way because I'm about to land. Euphoria. When just before the match West Ham took off their track suits to reveal their new Admiral kit I wasn't the least bit impressed, but now I didn't care. Half time is approaching lads, keep it tight and we'll go in one up, sweet. But then Frank Lampard hits a horrible back pass, its woefully short, it gets intercepted, they score and its 1-1 at half time. My thoughts go straight back to the League Cup Semi Final, it's Déjà Vu, John McDowell all over again but then again you knew I was going to write that. Immediately after half time they score once more and now we're up against it. Tricky Trev curls in an inviting cross for Keith Robson to head us level - now it's up for grabs. With fifteen minutes remaining West Ham concede a debatable penalty and they put it away, so we have to chase the game again. We push up and they breakaway to make it 4-2 (and a long way home). When Lampard under hit that back pass he injured himself and never returned for the second half, so Alan Taylor came on and the side was reorganised. I will always remember on the way out I saw this hammers fan, a real big guy sitting on a wall crying his eyes out. (I feel your pain fella.) We had been beaten but the team had given their all. The journey home after an away defeat always seemed to take an eternity.

We made our way back to the coach and the mood was very sombre. Our ferry crossing wasn't until the early hours of the next morning. The driver got a fair distance away from the stadium and told us he would be parking up but we didn't have to stay on the coach, I think I was the only person who wanted to stay on board. After seeing us get beaten, I was sick, gutted and any other cliché you care to name; I was in no mood for a jolly up. When everyone came back they told me they had found a bar/club and had a good time. Fair play to them, they wanted to enjoy themselves so good luck to them but I knew the way I was feeling I would have been lousy company. I replayed the match over in my mind a couple of times before eventually dropping off to sleep. When we finally got aboard the ferry there were tired and shattered West Ham boys all over the place. I too was tired and starving. I was so sleepy in fact I only went and ate the stick of West Ham rock which I wanted to keep (oh no). We arrived back in Basildon at midday. If nothing else I had learned a lesson from the Stoke City Cup Semi Final, I had booked the day off work, so went home and fell into bed.

# I've Been Here Before

By this time our Sunday league side E.S.L. were doing really well and we had won two promotions in the space of three seasons. My dad was still coming to watch every week as he had always done, whereas when it came to the Saturday side it would mainly be the home games he would attend. He got to know all the players in the E.S.L. side along with their family and friends who would stand on the touchline with him. Our manager at the time was a man called Ernie Dipple; all of us players got on well with him and enjoyed playing for him. So we were rather surprised when he told us that he wanted to step down as manager. Now, as my dad was a familiar face around the club it was suggested that he should take over; this idea came from some of the players initially. Without too much persuading he was happy to take on the role. Ernie's good work was much appreciated; dad just tweaked the team slightly by bringing in two or three more players. The plan was successful in as much as during the next two seasons we gained one more promotion.

By now we had eight West Ham fans in the side, how could we fail. One of our new additions was a fella called Johnny Martin; my first meeting with him was when we went to the Charity Shield game between West Ham and

Derby County at Wembley. There was a crowd of us going by coach and John suggested that we all chip in a certain amount and he would organise our 'liquid lunch'. The coach was due to leave Basildon at 10.30am, most of us arrive at about 10.15 and still no sign of Johnny and it's now departure time. We then asked the driver if it would be possible to wait a while longer which he agreed to and give us fifteen minutes more. Still there is no sign of Johnny and its 10.45! The driver wants to leave now, we then explain to him why we don't want to leave yet as he has all the beer which we had already paid for. To be fair to the driver he waited till 11.00am, by which time other passengers were demanding to go and so we did. We are now driving down the A127 on a really hot day with no 'dizzy water'. The people at the back then shout out that there is car behind constantly beeping his horn, flashing his lights and trying to get in front of us. It turned out to be Johnny; it was quite a sight to see him trying to get in front of us to stop the coach (I never had to do that on my test). His mission was eventually accomplished and the driver pulled over to let him on. We helped unload the beers onto the coach and his partner drove the car back home. The sun shone all day and we found a good home for the drinks alas, for the game we lost to the champions 2-0 and never really threatened them, but you can never get tired of seeing your team at Wembley.

John was a very good influence in the dressing room as he would always be chatting and keeping us amused with his stories. I don't think he had tonsils I think he had a fan-belt, how many of his tales were true is open to question. The one he would always want to retell was when at the end of a night out he ended up dancing with Princess Anne. Sunday morning football was so far removed back then it was untrue. We were playing a team called St. Basils, after the referee had blown his whistle for half time and their goalkeeper started to walk back to the dressing room. The opposing manager started to shout at him asking where he was going, the goalkeeper simply shouted back that he was going home for his dinner.

Steve Lloyd was now playing for E.S.L. on this occasion. He had headed the ball out of defence, he stopped in his tracks and shouted "Oh no". We gathered round thinking he was injured only for us to be told that his contact lens had fallen out. The referee stopped the game and suggested we (both teams) should get down on all fours and search for it, and unexpectedly someone actually found it.

When playing for an earlier Sunday League side the manager, who shall remain nameless, passed on some very confusing advice. It was blowing a gale that morning and we were about to kick into the teeth of a fearsome wind. So before we kick off the manager says and I quote "You've seen what the wind's doing out there today lads, so keep your high balls on the floor". He never did win manager of the month.

Apart from the football, Steve and I were still socialising on a regular basis. The first part of Friday evening we would be playing tennis, then out clubbing (no not seals) this would be a local club called Sweeney's. We enjoyed playing tennis as a doubles partnership; the opposition would be my dad and one of his mates which would be either Brian Carson or Dave Palmer. And dad's friends soon became our friends. Brian, the intelligent one, was a West Ham fan while Dave was a Tottenham supporter. He could take a joke about his team and was more than happy to give plenty back. So that was the Friday line-up, Steve and I against dad and either Brian or Dave. Even though Dave was a Spurs fan I went to a few of our battles with him and I would say things like "You've got the best team in the country, it's just in the towns you're not so clever". As luck would have it, most of the time the Irons did me proud and the journey home was a pleasant one. Dave got me tickets for the League Cup game at White Hart Lane in 75-76 and we got a 0-0 draw which I'm happy about, the hard work is done. Before the replay, the draw for the next round is made and it's Doncaster Rovers that await us, that'll do for me. Two words that spring to mind are hatch and chickens. Dave Palmer couldn't make the replay (phew) because we went and blew it at home, losing 2-0 after extra time and a floodlight failure. The home game in 71-72 against Spurs was another nightmare for Dave as Trevor Brooking and Ade Coker scored in a 2-0 victory. The goal Trevor scored was shown countless times on The Big Match, after turning the defender inside out (I think he went off with twisted blood) he curled one in the top corner. Pick that one out! Worse to come for Mr Palmer in season 83-84, this time he gets us seats in the Paxton Road upper tier. No matter wherever we sit I keep seeing the Hammers win, this time 2-0 with Whitton and Swindlehurst making for another happy car journey home. I went with Brian and his mates to Ipswich away in 1970, it seemed a postponement was in the offing as we drove through snow and it was a freezing cold day. The orange ball made an appearance for the match as we got beat 1-0. I really like both Brian and Dave and spent many happy hours in their company, the Friday tennis nights lasted for over three years.

The following season after playing my last game for Bowers, I went and joined up with Grays Athletic in the Athenian League. Not too long after joining them the manager left for pastures new and I was no longer enjoying my football which the new manager saw. Billy was still at Bowers and playing really well. A chap called Johnny Clarke, who had previous connections with Bowers, was to be taking charge of Billericay Town Reserves, myself and Billy were asked to go. Without hesitation Billy took up the offer and joined but I on the other hand had a more difficult decision to make. After being on the waiting list for seven years for a season ticket, one had finally become available to me. Should I play or should I go (I'm sure The Clash pinched that idea from me). What a decision, but I chose to go for the season ticket. For Billy it proved to be the right one because he progressed quickly to the first team as I expected he would. To cap off a fantastic season they won the F.A. Vase, he even got to play at Wembley. Not only was he an excellent player but also a good mate and fully deserved the success that came his way. For my part, I was more than happy how events would unfold for me.

# More Regular than Albran

It's season 77-78 and after my very long 'loan spell' the lads sign me on full time. Ian, Dave, Steve and Trevor welcome me to the ranks as a full time regular. Everyone has their own match day rituals and we would be no different. Dave was a lorry driver and would often work Saturday mornings, so Steve and I would take it in turns to drive to Dave's. We would pick up Trevor along the way while Ian would drive from Benfleet and we all then congregate at Dave's. On arrival Dave's wife Brenda would provide tea and biscuits to make us welcome. Now Dave had a passion for collecting West Ham scrapbooks, he not only bought the national newspapers but also the Stratford Express, Romford Recorder and any other edition carrying articles on the Hammers. He cut out and collected match reports, pictures, items of gossip and general interest on our heroes. So while we were waiting for Dave, Brenda would let us have a catch up reading his latest handy work. I think I am right in saying that eventually this collection would get out of hand, he had so many all over the house until they had no more storage space left and Dave ended up giving them all away.

So Dave arrives home and we're ready for the off, Ian would always drive to home games in his Citroen which was a beautiful car, really comfortable and roomy. He worked for the Pearl Insurance Company and went to home games dressed smartly with some insurance related paperwork visible on the dashboard. We would jump out at Barking Road (sometimes he would even stop to let us do this). He would then go on to park in Priory Road, which was right outside the east stand. If at any time a policeman questioned his right to park there, he was an insurance agent working in the area. This was great for us, for when the game finished we were ideally placed for a quick getaway. Sometimes we would go to the Boleyn but not always. What did become a ritual was the walk into Green Street, this would be after Trevor and I had found somewhere to give our money to the sick animals. Mind you, we didn't know they were sick when we went into Ladbrokes to back them.

Steve was fanatical about collecting programmes both home and away, always ensuring there were no gaps in his collection. So, in Green Street we would search out the guy who had all the back dated issues. Then for Dave we had to go to the stall that sold the metal lapel badges. He enjoyed collecting those, and even if the fella had no new stock he was always willing to chat about all things claret and blue. My personal preference was the stall with the T-shirts that had slogans printed on them. Come rain or shine we would adhere to this routine, the only down side was when we went in to the ground we were not all together. Dave and Trevor favoured the South Bank, Steve and Ian had seats in the East stand, but not together and I was over in the West stand. With us all watching from different viewing points this made for interesting post match discussions on the journey home. One of the main reasons for my preference for away games is that we are all watching the match standing together.

I had always worn the same pair of jeans for matches. These had many West Ham patches sewn on to them, purchased from a stall in Green Street. Each one of the patches had a slogan printed on them. Some examples to describe them were as follows: next to West Ham I like sex best, West Ham turn me on, West Ham rule, super irons, and West Ham are magic. Another had a giant claret fist saying mighty West Ham. Anyway as I said these were my chosen attire for match days, and now a season ticket holder saw no reason to change. When I took my seat for the first time I was also wearing my claret and blue hooped rugby shirt. I received quite a few glances, although not too many seemed to be of the admiring kind. Where I was sitting apart from the odd scarf there was little evidence of club colours. It's not a great start to my life as a season ticket holder as we suffer a 3-1 defeat to Norwich City. Up front John Radford fails to impress me and if only I had a pound for every time I have said that. It would be results like that which were to cause our own private little sweepstake to rollover. Every game we went to we would each predict the score and then pay in a certain amount. I cannot remember the exact cost of the entry fee, only knowing that it was nothing too extravagant to break the bank. I wasn't Jewish but I was saving up to be. The predictions were written on a piece of paper, and along with the money were placed in the glove compartment of Ian's car. Was it the sense of miss-placed loyalty, but our selections defied all sense of logic when trying to win money. We were going to every game hoping to see West Ham win so our predictions reflected this. Obviously if nobody had the correct score the money would rollover. But alas, even if you were lucky enough to have foreseen the outcome you still didn't win as such. That would be because at the next game it may have been said for example "Ian you won the predictor last week the milky bars are on you". That being the case I would suggest the most successful winner would have been the Boleyn pub.

Another reason as to why I enjoyed the away games was because the journey more often than not was a laughter filled ride. The banter was great and all the lads could take a joke and no offence was ever intended or taken. I'm sure that is one of the reasons why we are all still friends to this day.

Our next home game was against Manchester City and we get beat again. Now I am sitting there thinking have I put a 'jinx' on things by having a season ticket. Hindsight is a wonderful thing. From that opening day defeat in August I will have to wait until the middle of December before witnessing a home victory. In amongst so many frustrating home performances Trevor Brooking earns a well deserved testimonial game. We take on an England X1 and win a very entertaining affair 6-2. Hammers fans turn out in numbers to show their appreciation for one of our finest sons. We have signed Derek Hales from Charlton so now Pop Robson has some support up front, and we are now scoring a few more goals. Our patchy form has done nothing to dampen our optimism, be positive, chin up; we can get out of this. (I lie so convincingly.) Going to Q.P.R. in an F.A. cup replay only serves to pile on more misery as we are creamed 6-1. I am convinced this is part of our masterplan to leave us free to concentrate on the league. It is now mid March and Wolves are the visitors for a game we must win, as they are just above us in the table. Sticking to the usual routine we emerge from the Boleyn pub. Outside is a seafood stall and Dave approaches the young lady who is serving. He then enquires "do you have crabs?" She replies with a yes and Dave's response is "well wash your hands and get me some prawns". By five o'clock we had recorded yet another home defeat and now we are really in the brown stuff. I don't think even Derren Brown can get us out of this one.

Because I had been previously playing on Saturdays I had missed a lot of games with the lads. So hearing about their escapades would make me smile, even if West Ham couldn't. The story of Norwich away was certainly an eventful one. This trip was by coach and the boys needed a stop to answer the call of nature. The driver pulled in at a lay by whereupon the lads went into a field. Trevor and Dave said that there must have been about twenty of them. Finishing first Dave noticed two large boxes and proceeded to kick them. These would turn out to be no ordinary boxes, for when Dave kicked them hundreds of bees came swarming out. They said it was so funny to see all these guys trying to hurry up and put away 'their best friend' before it got stung, and a mad dash back to the coach followed.

Another episode occurred away at Southampton in the F.A. cup. We had won this tie 2-1 and Dave was making his way out of the ground when he noticed on the ground a set of keys. They were very distinctive and also had what appeared to be a security key on them. After picking them up he handed them in to a police officer. Later when they get off at Waterloo train station a man is looking on the floor of the platform and turning his pockets inside out. Dave asked him if he had a problem and the guy said that he had lost his keys. On hearing this Dave enquired if they had a security key on them and went on to describe the other keys and the key fob. The man's face lit up as he was so pleased on hearing this news. "Have you got them?" he asked. "No", said Dave "I gave them to a copper in Southampton". The poor guy was crestfallen, one minute you're top of the world and then-.

So now I am in a better mood and what do you know, West Ham get their act together and go on a decent run. Playing eight games we win six and only lose two. Sylvester Stallone, Michael Caine, Bobby Moore, Pele come on we can do this. (Escape to victory, now do you get it.) Last game of the season is at home to Liverpool, a win and we are safe, no problem. Well I can tell you now that sticking to pre match rituals, wearing the lucky pants, wearing the lucky shirt-they don't work and god knows I've tried that system enough times. A 2-0 defeat and we are on the way home checking out the routes to Luton, Cambridge and other magnificent stadiums.

# We'll be Back

West Ham are no longer a division one team, and E.S.L. are no longer a team. We had climbed up to the premier division in the Basildon Sunday league and the games were much tougher. Three of our players had chosen to hang up their boots and call it a day. One moved away and two had work commitments and so it was a sad day when the team folded. Where is a Chinese billionaire when you need one? I had many happy memories from my time with that team, both on and off the pitch. Social events were organised to raise money for club funds and a good time was had by one and all. Birthdays and anniversaries were also celebrated which went a long way to help with the team bonding. It was my pleasure to play with such a great bunch of lads.

Steve and I went to play for Fryerns F.C. and once again landed on our feet. A well run club with four teams playing in the Basildon Sunday league, with plenty of good lads and more than their fair share of talented individuals.

After my first year as a season ticket holder this time round it would definitely not be a case of "the difficult second album", it just had to be better. Even though we have been relegated the loyalty of the fans would never be questioned. If we never had a game I'm sure we could get 25,000 turning up just to watch the grass grow. The season gets under way and it's raining goals. Five at home to Notts County and three away in midweek at Newcastle. "The famous five" (Steve, Ian, Dave, Trevor and I) agree to go to Selhurst Park for the Crystal Palace game. We are going along a road in Croydon high street and the traffic is at a snail's pace. We came to a halt beside a bus stop which was in front of a Radio Rental's television shop. Dave opened his window and said to a man who was standing in the bus queue " would you mind moving out of the way I'm trying to watch this programme", and much to our surprise he did move out of the way. He must have thought we were going to park there for ages.

On arrival at the ground there is a heavy police presence. Steve is walking on his own about twenty yards in front of us. A nearby policeman has a lively Alsation on a lead, and it is barking loudly, rearing on its back legs and dribbling from the mouth. Deciding to give this ferocious animal a wide berth Steve then walks off a straight line, and arc's his walk into a semi circle to avoid the dog. Dave quietly creeps up behind him grab's a handful of flesh at the back of Steve's thigh and start's barking loudly like a dog. It was the fastest I had seen Steve move for ages. As for the game itself Alan Taylor scores and it ends all square 1-1, yeah we'll settle for that. Steve and I miss the next two matches as we are on holiday in Benidorm. We have gone with six of the lads from Fryerns F.C, as we are doing missionary work teaching the locals "El Bubbles". We have somehow found ourselves drinking in a bar where the radio is tuned in to the world service. They have live second half commentary on West Ham versus Burnley. In the time we are listening we ship in two goals and our 2-1 half time lead is now just a distant memory.

Back home our good form inspires us to go to Leicester, although it wasn't raining it might as well have been. As usual we were behind the goal but on this occasion their lot were right above us. All they wanted to do was keep spitting down on us, and as usual the police did nothing. Two goal David Cross provides us with three points and a merry little journey home. Boxing Day's home fixture sends Orient our way along with another rude awakening. Not only do we get beat but our former goalkeeper Mervyn Day keeps a clean sheet, well he would wouldn't he. Travelling home we all air our opinions as to why and where it's all going wrong. To us it is so obvious; the only thing baffling us is why we have never been invited to sit on the board! So Steve refers to happier times and reminds us of the day at Ipswich. The road was packed with loads of hammers fans making their way to the stadium and a bakers van is trying to reverse out. Banging on the side of the van Dave then lies down in the road by the back wheel. The driver jumps out in a panic, sees Dave lying there and thinks he has knocked him down. With a face as white as a ghost he pleads "sorry mate I didn't see you, are you o.k." Dave looked up gave a wink and replied "got any cakes mate".

It wasn't as if we were not getting enough of our hammers fix, but I organised another trip anyway. This was to the empire pool Wembley for the Evening Standard five a sides. There had previously been on television a midweek show called Sportsnight with Coleman. This programme had covered the tournament before and I can remember us winning it a couple of times. The likes of Bonds, Sissons, Hurst, Howe, and Clive Charles were prominent in those triumphant days. I booked the transport and quite a few lads from Fryerns came. The atmosphere was good even while waiting for the late arrivals to join up. One of whom climbed aboard only to say sorry for being late but he had just let his girlfriend down. Another voice from the back was heard to reply, never mind you can blow her up again tomorrow. A draw had been made and it was a straight knockout competition. Eagerly we awaited the arrival of our hero's only for them to go out in round one. We then have to sit and watch the rest of the competition with little or no interest. This is the second time I have been and we went out early that time too. Clyde

Best played then, now I did like him but he was never built for the nippy five a side game. This type of tournament would be a forerunner for the masters six a side events. After going on two occasions and having seen the hammers play for probably no more than half an hour I won't be organising any more of these trips.

The next away outing we embark on is down to the south coast to Brighton. Some of the West Ham boys had travelled down the night before and had caused trouble during the evening, because of this when we get near to Brighton the police have coned off the road to force us into single file traffic. This is to enable them to stop every car and do a search. Memories come flooding back to a previous time when I got stopped by the boys in blue. I was driving and four of us lads from the E.S.L. team were on our way to a club in Canvey Island on a Saturday night. The flashing blue lights persuaded me to pull over, and the officer invited me to step out. Upon doing this he then turned to me and said "you're staggering". To which I replied "you're not so bad yourself". Back to the story, the police searches have now made us late and we are fighting the clock. We get outside the ground and we can't find a space to park, double yellow lines everywhere and lots of police in attendance. It's five to three and a big roar goes up and we are still outside as the teams take to the field. Ian spots a courtyard, no yellow lines and an empty space. He says to the officer "can we park there?" To which the constable replied with a firm no. Pointing to the already parked cars Ian says "what about them". He responded "they didn't ask" and calmly walked off. By now we were past caring and did not want to miss more of the game, so we all jumped out and left the car parked on double yellows. On our return we had two parking tickets. We split the cost five ways and gave our money to Ian. Pop Robson scores twice, we win 2-1, and the world is a much better place.

For most of the season we have been threatening near the top of the league which encourages us to venture on our travels once again. Next on our hit list is Luton Town for a mid-week encounter. It is our first chance to get to see our new goalkeeper big Phil Parkes. We are not to be disappointed as he appears to be an inspiration to the defence. I felt it to be a great shame how previous goalkeeper Mervyn Day's time with us ended. He had a couple of wonderful years giving the impression we had a quality keeper for the next few seasons. When he first burst onto the scene as a teenager he was so impressive, even winning the F.A. young player of the year. Ron Greenwood once remarked that he would be West Ham's goalkeeper for the next ten years. Unfortunately he suffered a loss of confidence and errors became commonplace and it all went Pete Tong. He must have known the writing was on the wall when they were going to put a bell inside the ball so he knew when it was coming.

I digress, we are back on the road to Luton and Ian is driving with Dave in the passenger seat. Steve, Trevor and I are sitting in the back. Trevor was tapping Dave on the back of the head and finding one of Ian's tools began to rap him on the back of his hand which unsurprisingly wasn't going down at all well with Dave, who told Trevor to pack it in. I never realised that Trevor had a death wish but he regarded Dave's annoyance as something of a challenge and carried on. All of a sudden Dave swung round this huge fist which Trevor avoided. It was coming straight for me and at first I thought he was offering me a banana by the size of it. Now had he hit the door or the window he could have done himself some serious damage. So it was very lucky for him that I stopped it with my eye. It wouldn't be too long before I had an eye to match the claret and blue on my scarf. When I got home my dad thought that the Luton fans must have objected to my rendition of bubbles being slightly off key. I always said I could take Dave with one eye closed, now was my chance to prove it (just my little joke Dave-honest).

Being season ticket holders offered me and Steve the advantage of free entry to reserve games. We took up this offer and went to a fair few games. I enjoyed these games as it gave us a chance to view up and coming young players trying to prove they were worth a place in the first team. There was also the prospect of seeing any previously injured players returning to action. Putting out a strong side tended to be the norm. Unlike modern times all the reserve matches took place at Upton Park. Also we would include some youth cup games on our scouting missions. The kids made it to the final of the F.A. Youth Cup and we went to see the first leg of the final at home to Ipswich Town. The visitors were far too good on the night and fully deserved their 3-1 victory. They went on to win the second leg as well to take the trophy. In our ranks that evening we saw the young Alvin Martin, Geoff Pike, Alan Curbishley and Paul Brush all of whom would go on to have good career's in the game. The famous five go to Cambridge and the crowd is restricted to 11,000. It's a small old ground but there appears to be hammers fans everywhere. A 0-0 draw is not a great result for us as we are beginning to slip off the pace. Riding on the crest of a slump still cannot curb our enthusiasm and we are all raring to go for the short trip across town to Orient. Our loyalty was not misplaced (was it ever) and we are duly rewarded with a comfortable 2-0 win. It was worth the admission money alone just to witness Geoff Pike's 'worldie'. 'Stupid boy' never scored that many goals but when he does decide to hit one it's more often than not a collector's item, a home win against Cardiff is now essential, so in typical fashion West Ham go and draw. We return to the car and realise that our promotion ship has been waved off at the quayside. Comments range from "that's it I'm finished, I'm not going any more", to "they'll never get another penny of my money". By the time we reach Basildon the question is raised of who is going to the Burnley game and it is met with a positive response, we all are. Just what is it with you West Ham; we just can't seem to stay mad at you for long. No wins from our final four games and we're going nowhere-or rather I am.

# I've Met My Match

There were three of us in this marriage now and they were me, my love for West Ham and my love for playing. I had given up hope waiting for John Radford to score a goal. It's a pity he never had six shots at John Lennon as then he'd still be alive today. What was it, something like thirty odd games without a goal which isn't too clever for a centre forward. Mind you had we gone ahead and signed Zaza I'm confident he could have beaten that with his 'moon river' shots (wider than a mile.) At this point in the proceedings I chose to play for Basildon Town in the Southend league. I would still meet up with the lads on a Friday night at Sweeney's. Added to the fact a few of the boys from my Sunday side Fryerns would be there the evenings were always a good laugh. One such evening would be memorable in more ways than one as it was the evening that changed my life, and for the better I might add. I was having a pint with Steve: it only takes one pint to get him drunk (it's normally the fourteenth.)

I had noticed a beautiful girl and went over and asked if she wanted to dance. Luckily for me she agreed and during the dance she told me her name was Marie. She was so easy to talk to; I wanted to see her again. I got her phone number, called and asked if I could take her to the pictures (and no, this wasn't one of those heavy breathing calls!) Still my luck was holding out and we went to see our first film together. This was The Goodbye Girl staring Richard Dreyfuss. See Marie it's not just West Ham facts I can remember, I can also remember the important things too. It was a good film and we began to go out together on a regular basis. This was in season 78-79 when I was a season ticket holder so away games wouldn't always allow me to get back for Saturday nights out. Now that I was playing on Saturdays I was able to take Marie out more.

On the odd occasion she came to watch me play on a Sunday morning. Things were going really well in our relationship and I already knew that she was the one for me. Most parents tend to know when their son is serious about a girl if he brings her home to meet them. Well my parents knew I was serious about Marie because I was taking her to meet **my** West Ham. I had never taken a girlfriend to West Ham before or ever wanted to for that matter, but Marie was special (and still is.) I wanted her to love West Ham as much as I did; only I did not want her love affair with West Ham to be 'a one night stand'. So for that reason there was going to be no waiting on cold platforms for a train that when having arrived you can't get a seat. No queuing down the side of Upton Park station. No standing on the North Bank with tiny steps and some 'Greggs-on-legs' bloke blocking the view.

For all of the above reasons I made the decision to drive us to the game. A nice warm car journey and entry to the East stand lower with the large steps. I've done my bit West Ham, now don't you let me down. All you've got to do is play champagne football, score a few goals, and we've won the heart of the fair maiden. I wasn't with the lads but the goal celebrations were far more enjoyable with Marie. Another reason for viewing from the East stand was that it made for a quick getaway back to the car. This would have been parked in either Kimberley Avenue or Mafeking Avenue. The plan was a success and Marie came with me on many nights to watch the hammers and I was so happy she did.

We had planned to get married and preparations began, there was so much to do. Booking the church, and the reception, photographer, disco etc. it was a hectic time. Even though we were saving up for the wedding we still found time to go out regularly. Wednesday night would be our ten-pin bowling night, quite often we would take Marie's sister Karen and her brother Stephen.

My Sunday side Fryerns would regularly have functions raising money for club funds. The fancy dress nights were always popular and well supported. They each had different themes for example there was vicars and tarts, a tramps supper and television programmes. For the television programme's night Marie dressed up as an angel and I was the devil, we were upstairs-downstairs, that's one for all you older readers. The best one was a woman who turned up wearing nothing but a pair of black gloves, and black stilettos. She said she had come as the five of spades. O.K. so I may have made that bit up but the upstairs-downstairs was true.

There were still more wedding preparations to take care of. Flowers, honeymoon, presents for the mums and dads, best man and bridesmaids all still needed to be arranged. My circle of friends was ever widening but there was only ever one person I wanted to be my best man, and I was so pleased when Steve agreed. Still fresh in the memory is the moment when I proposed to Marie. I got down on one knee and said those famous four little words "you're not are you?" Dear reader I jest having never said that. The traditional will you marry me is what I opted for. Marie still wanted me to ask for her parent's permission which I was more than happy to do. Just because we are saving up for our wedding doesn't mean that we have stopped socialising. Dad's sister Nell and her husband Arthur both work at S.T.C. and they have regular variety shows and dances. These are family shows consisting of singers, comedians and speciality acts. The tickets are always reasonably priced and the venue is only a ten minute drive away. My favourite night was in 1975 and West Ham had been victorious in the cup final after beating Fulham 2-0. We went a function as usual at S.T.C. and on our arrival discovered much to our delight that the F.A. cup was on display. For a small fee it was possible to have your picture taken with the cup, and I wasn't going to miss out on such a golden opportunity as this. I was overjoyed to get my hands on the trophy and looking back at the picture now, I notice that my knuckles are white as I was gripping it so tightly.

By playing football on Saturdays will not completely rule me out from getting to Upton Park. This is down to the boys showing great form in both the league cup and the F.A. cup. Marie and I get to see six games between the two competitions. Undoubtedly the highlight was going all the way to Wembley for the final of the F.A. cup. About a month before the final we were desperately hoping Billy Bonds would be available. An evening fixture saw us at home to Birmingham City. I took Marie along to further her education in the finer points of British culture. Roughly mid-way through the second half Bill gets involved in a bit of a scrap with Colin Todd and both players are sent off. Quite easily Bill could have been banned and missed the final. Like many hammers fans I was forever checking the press and the radio for the outcome of the decision by the Football Association. Thankfully dame fortune was smiling upon us, the decision went in Bill's favour and he would be there to lead us out. So

Bill is going to be there now all I've got to do is somehow get myself there. I'm not a season ticket holder anymore so it could be seen that I have left, and West Ham get to Wembley. Due to this fact I think it is safe to say I'm suffering from what could be known as 'Pop Robson syndrome'. In past days a season ticket holder was guaranteed a ticket for the final, this time around I've got my work cut out.

We are due to play Arsenal in a London derby so tickets are going to be at a premium. I say at a premium, when what I really mean is that they are about as rare as rocking horse shit. My dad saw one advertised in the local paper and the cost was a week's wages which he thought was a bit steep. I don't know about steep, I thought it was more like vertical. In 1975 I managed to get a cup final ticket via the lucky programme system. Not having been to many games, this time round I was unsure if that was still an option. Had it been my decision I would have given a ticket to all those who turned up for the evening fixture against Cambridge United just before Christmas. I had planned to take Marie but the weather took a turn for the worse. Mid afternoon the snow came down rather heavily and was settling fast, (these days I like it when it snows, because then my garden looks as good as everybody else's) added to the fact it was now getting quite foggy. I suggested that the match wouldn't go ahead and that we should give it a miss. After all I didn't want to brave the elements and then arrive at the ground only to find the match had been postponed. I got that all wrong and the game went ahead. It was reported that fans who were behind the goals could not see to the other end of the ground, so when a goal was scored they would sing out the name of the goal scorer. We won the game 3-1 and I would give a ticket to each and every one of those brave and loyal fans who turned up.

Every year Fryerns F.C. would automatically get two cup final tickets from the Essex F.A. Players from all four of our teams could put their names into the 'lucky draw' to win them. Most years I wouldn't bother putting my name in because if West Ham weren't going to be there, then neither was I. Naturally this time my name was included and the draw took place at the clubhouse on a Friday night a couple of weeks before the final. I was unable to attend the draw but nonetheless my prayers are answered and I am the winner. It was customary to draw a second name to cover the eventuality of the winner being unable to go; therefore a standby was in place. This procedure was completed and the standby was Johnny Burnett who was also a fanatical hammers fan. He was told he was first reserve in case I couldn't use them. I think his reply was something along the lines of SOME HOPE (and I've cleaned that up.) Panic over, and I'm now the proud owner of two cup final tickets. "Dad I'm taking you to Wembley" had such a lovely sound to it. The lads were also lucky enough to get tickets but were at the opposite end of the stadium to us. Being a division below Arsenal makes us the underdogs, but we are a second division team in name only. The team is first class and so are the fans. The famous five have arranged to meet that evening at the Castle Mayne pub in Basildon. A magical day see's us destroy the gunners 1-0; we rose to the occasion on the day that saw Arsenal rarely threaten. It wasn't until meeting up with the lads that night I found out they never knew who had scored the goal, as they were positioned behind the goal at the opposite end to where Trevor Brooking headed the winner in the thirteenth minute. We were deserving of the trophy after a fabulous all round team performance. Yes it was 1-0 to us and to be frank Arsenal were lucky to get nil. After the final we returned to our coach, before setting off the driver asked the question "do you want to go back home via West Ham and see the celebrations?" The loudest voices went for the yes option. My resounding NO just got lost in amongst it all. I didn't want to sit on a coach watching others celebrate; I wanted to get home as soon as possible and do my own celebrating with my friends and family. As I am sure you can imagine the traffic was horrendous. Eventually we are nearing Upton Park, coming close to Green Street from Forest Gate. Traffic now is at a standstill, people are sitting on their cars, others are continually blowing their horns and crowds are dancing in the street. All this is great but I just want to get home. I explained to dad I'd had enough and got off the coach and ran to Upton Park station to get the train home. Mum had saved my evening meal for me but I explained to her that I had no time to eat as I had promised to pick Marie up and we had to meet up with the lads at the pub. My dad too became tired of sitting on the coach and was on the next train behind mine. I'm now way behind schedule and with great haste collect Marie and we go to the pub where the others have already arrived. We had one drink and a chat with the lads and their better halves whereupon I informed Marie that we were leaving. When she asked why I told her we were on Match of the Day and I wanted to see it again. I don't think she was too pleased with me, taking the trouble to get ready and waiting so long for me to arrive all for just one drink. But when the hammers are on the telly sacrifices have to be made!

# **Those Are the Breaks**

We get off to a dodgy start in season 1980-81 whereby we have to wait until the fourth match to gain a victory, but the next thirteen games provide eleven wins and two draws (now this is what I signed up for.) I am still playing on Saturdays but it is still reassuring to know that the lads can still 'turn it on' without me having to be there to tell them how to go about it. I had previously persuaded Marie to come to Upton Park and we would go on a tour of the ground. We (or should that be I) had been eagerly waiting to see the photo's we had taken, and they did not disappoint. There was one of Marie standing alone in the middle of the north bank, even the I.C.F. kept well out of her way. We had pictures taken in the dressing room and other parts of the ground. Without question my favourite was the one with us both lifting the F.A. cup.

This time around I don't get to go to many games as we depart from the F.A. cup at the first hurdle. Not to worry I'm still thinking positively we have after all got European football to look forward to. The first round requires us to travel to Spain to play Castilla, a game that was marred by crowd trouble both inside and outside of the stadium. On top of a 3-1 defeat our punishment for our part in the trouble was to play the second leg at home behind closed doors. It was a strange atmosphere with no crowd present; it was so quiet it was just like being at Highbury. Extra time was required to despatch the Spaniards to the tune of 5-1 as we march into the next round.

Our journey in the European Cup Winners Cup continues and I attend the first leg of the tie with the Rumanian side Politechnic Timisoara, and witness a comfort able 4-0 win. We can also afford the luxury of Ray Stewart missing a penalty as there seems little danger of us going out to this lot. It doesn't matter we are beaten 1-0 away because our name is safely in the hat for yet another draw. I go to the matches against Burnley and Barnsley in the league cup and that's it for the season for reasons why I will explain later.

Marie and I were still enjoying our evenings out with the family mainly because the shows were always crowd pleasers at the S.T.C. social club. They too ventured into fancy dress nights and the one that we went along to was an open theme. I had plenty of help from Marie with regard to my costume and make-up. She bandaged my head gave me a black eye (not literally) and made it appear as though I had cuts and bruises on my face with blood everywhere. I borrowed a set of crutches and my foot was bandaged to give the impression that it was broken. My trousers were torn and I wore a plain white T-shirt. Printed on the shirt in large letters were the words SOD HER AND HER MILK

TRAY. That is yet another one for you older readers, there ought to have been a stewards enquiry as I didn't win, is there no justice!

By now I had been 'preaching the gospel' so well that Marie's sister Karen and brother Stephen joined us for a couple of games which were quite memorable. Because of my own playing commitments we decided to make the most of pre-season friendlies, and one of the regular ones would be at Southend United. So the four of us went along and it was my suggestion in order to avoid any trouble we shouldn't go behind the goal. My instinct told me we should be safer on the side opposite the player's tunnel which at first seemed to be the correct choice. This was to be the calm before the storm as once we scored then it all kicked off. Bottles were being thrown, fighting amongst both sets of fans police intervention and we had to make ourselves scarce.

The second one was a testimonial for Billy Bonds at Upton Park against Spurs and we scored four and a job well done, it is always good to get one over on Spurs in any form of competition. This was played on November 5th and it was a mission dodging the firework's that were being thrown on the journey back to the car. Overall a good night, but as far as testimonials go I preferred the one for Geoff Hurst against a European X1. To witness such greats as Eusebio, Seeler and all the other international players who gave their time made for a wonderful evening ending in a 4-4 draw.

Having to plan the wedding so far in advance I didn't allow for West Ham to win the F.A. cup and therefore book their place for a return visit in the charity shield. So now it turns out I'm to be married on the day the hammers are playing at Wembley. The way my luck is when my ship comes in I will be at the airport. But hold on let's get this into perspective; the most wonderful girl I know is going to marry me so life is pretty good after all. It was to be a 4 p.m. wedding and West Ham were kicking off at 3p.m. so I asked Marie to wait and find out the half time score before leaving for the church. Then when she came down the aisle she would be able to let me know how we were doing. It was a glorious day and I didn't know what true happiness was until I got married (and then it was too late.) Not really she has been brilliant and I could not have wished for a better wife. The hall for the reception was decorated in claret and blue, the cake had claret and blue ribbons on it and the D.J. brought with him a copy of 'bubbles'. The two dads and I, best man Steve and Marie's brother Stephen all had special claret and blue flowers for our buttonholes. When Steve made his speech he produced a 'good luck on your wedding day' card signed by all the West Ham cup final team. This was due in no small way to my brother-in-law Ted who approached Pat Holland for some help. Trevor had been the usher for us at our wedding but nevertheless it still went well. Returning from honeymoon we joined the council waiting list for our first home.

There would be another wedding to look forward to in a few months' time as Marie's brother Stephen was to be married. For me there were always nights out with the boys as we are all close friends and life is grand. On the day of Stephen's wedding my Saturday side Basildon Town had a local derby versus Basildon B.C which I did not want to miss. We were top of the league and the goals had been flying in for me so I went to the ceremony but left the reception early to play in the match. It was in the second half with the score standing at 0-0 when I attempted to volley an effort at goal. The defender tried to block my shot and we clashed, I heard a crack and instantly knew that I had broken my leg, the blinding pain also gave me a clue. No blame was attached to the defender as it was a complete accident; the date was December 13th unlucky for some eh. On arrival at the hospital it was confirmed I had a double fracture of the left leg. This would be the second time I had broken this leg as it had happened when I was training with Fryerns and that time it caused me to miss out on playing in a cup final.

My leg was put in a full length cast from toe to thigh. Whilst lying on the bed and feeling sorry for myself the nurse came round and said "would you like a bed pan?" I then replied "What have I got to do my own cooking as well". So now my season for playing and watching was over. A broken leg is not going to stop me from enjoying the festive season. Friends give me a lift propped up on the back seat of their cars and we can go to our pre-arranged functions organised by the football club. At least I won't be missing out on the Boxing Day fixture as we are away this year. This was one game I always looked forward to when we are at home, either taking my dad or going with the lads. Nowadays it feels like all I am doing is studying for an A-level in cross words and word searches. I'm watching television all day and if it wasn't for Emmerdale Farm I wouldn't be getting any fresh air at all. So there I am stretched out on the sofa, leg propped up and feeling bored when all of a sudden there's a ring at the doorbell. Mum goes to answer it and walks back in accompanied by brother-in-law Ted and Pat Holland and at once my mood is lifted. What a surprise, I was expecting Trevor Brooking (no of course I wasn't.) It was a genuine thrill to meet Pat Holland he was great to talk to and seemed concerned as to how I was coping, but all I wanted to chat about was Pat and the hammers. He didn't arrive empty handed as he brought me a book on the championship winning season signed by all the squad with a get well message and I won't be parting with that. He told me that we would meet again which was nice of him but I thought no more of it. This season was Pat's testimonial year and various pubs over Essex were helping to raise money for him. In appreciation of their efforts Pat was delivering signed footballs to the publicans. He said that if I wanted to that it would be alright for me to spend some time going round with him, a lovely gesture and was gratefully accepted. He was so down to earth it was a pleasure to be in his company. Pat had large jars of tickets that were being sold in the pubs to boost his funds. These tickets had three windows on them and when opened they would reveal fruit symbols; these would be Cherries, Oranges Lemons etc. It was possible to win one of the various cash prizes if your ticket revealed one of the winning combinations, of which three cherries was the top award. I said to Pat that I would take a jar and try to sell some to family and friends. Whilst I was off work sick I took the jar with me when calling in to visit my workmates and they proved to be very popular. For helping him out Pat said I could be paid in cash or have a West Ham football signed by the players.

My best man Steve was due to be married soon and I was asked to be his best man, it was an honour to be asked so my positive reply was a real 'no brainer'. Marie and I had already bought the wedding present for Steve and Viv but I thought a signed ball would also go down well on the day. So I chose the ball instead of the cash and true to his word Pat delivered the goods. I had been working hard on my speech and other best man duties as I didn't want to let him down. My plan was to hand over the ball at the end of my speech and hopefully finish on a high. Over the years my dad had watched the pair of us grow up and he really liked Steve. So unbeknown to me he had written a poem and told me to read it out just before giving the ball to Steve. Below is the finished product I read out on his behalf (thanks dad).

*Dave and Steve have been hammers fans*
*Ever since they were quite small*
*They've seen them rise right to the top*
*And sometimes have seen them fall*
*But on this joyous occasion*
*Taking place inside this hall*
*It gives me the greatest of pleasure*
*To say to Steve from Dave this ball*

Well as I have mentioned earlier I would be unable to get to many league cup matches in that superb run to the final. Having now met Pat he promised to get me a ticket for the final. Yet again he delivered, but the only problem was that it was a standing ticket for behind the goal and I was still on crutches. He wasn't to know I would still be on crutches at that time, and even though I never got to Wembley I will always be thankful for the effort he put in on my behalf trying to get me there. This did have a happy ending as Pat managed to come up with tickets for me and Ted to go to Upton Park to see the Wrexham game when we clinch the Division 2 title with a 1-0 win. Once the full time whistle had been blown he took us into the players bar for a drink, where we had the opportunity to chat to a couple of the players. Yes Pat Holland will always be on my list of all time greats. This had been a record breaking season for points gained and goals scored as we romped away with the title. Suffering just four defeats all season this squad was the best I had ever seen.

# Back in the Old Routine

When the plaster came off my leg I was booked in for physiotherapy sessions at the hospital. The guy who would be taking care of me was called Mr. Fashanu, no not that one but he was just as big. I was determined to get back playing again, and three months of hard work meant I was ready to start training again. Still playing for Fryerns I started off on the comeback trail in the fourth team aiming to climb back to the first eleven. On Saturdays it was all change again as Basildon Town joined a different league which involved a lot more travelling. For that reason alone I chose to leave and in an ironic kind of a way I signed for Basildon B.C, the team I was playing against when I broke my leg. It was to become a decision I would be glad that I made after having two happy seasons with them. We never won a trophy but the football was good and the lads were first class. Our home ground was only ten minutes from my home which was another huge plus for me. I believed we were unlucky not to win anything as we were always close to the honours.

Before the new season was due to get underway we had a family wedding to go to. This was in Catford and as there were quite a few of us attending a mini-bus was booked. On the way the driver switched the radio on for the sports news, and we heard the presenter announce that the game between Sunderland and West Ham was going to be the live second half commentary choice. With the ceremony over we came out of the church for the photographs, only I made my way back to the mini-bus to listen to the second half with the driver. A single strike from Gary Rowell sends us home empty handed. I'm still with Marie so I think I'm forgiven.

Our first Saturday game wasn't until mid September so I was free to take dad to the home game versus Birmingham City. A 5-0 win provided great entertainment, if only it could be like this every week. The next month Basildon B.C. had a fixture called off and wouldn't you just know it the irons were at home. And it was not just any old home game it was the visit of the mighty Liverpool. During this period they really were the 'poodle's undercarriage', but we can play a bit too when we feel like it. We took them apart to the tune of 3-I, I just love it when a plan comes together. My dad and I had witnessed eight goals in two games and I am wondering whether to invest in a calculator or is that tempting fate. This was a superb little run with five wins on the bounce, seventeen goals scored, and we have beaten Liverpool, Arsenal and Manchester City all in the space of five weeks.

Marie wasn't going to games any more as by now we had our own home and said she had better ways of spending her time (totally impossible I know). For the remainder of the season I have to rely on the media to keep me up to date with events at Upton Park, because playing regularly restricts me to just one more visit. This was a league cup tie against Notts County. No trouble here cruising to a 3-0 win only to draw Liverpool away and we exit at the quarter final stage. The year 1983 was extra special to us as we are blessed with the arrival of our lovely daughter Melissa and West Ham's fan base increases by one. She was born on Friday the 13th but it's been our good luck to have her in our life. On the following day I drove to the hospital to bring Marie and Melissa home, and on the journey put the radio on. The commentary was Coventry versus West Ham and I'm driving home listening to a 4-2 win with my wife and new daughter and I'm really enjoying life now. It has become a tough decision as I am torn between playing and going to the Boleyn Ground with the lads, this was a thread constantly running through my life. Football with

Fryerns F.C. on Sundays is still featuring heavily in my life so I opt to quit playing on Saturdays.

I have never known a start to a campaign quite like this one, played five won five, scored fifteen conceded three. Having given up my season ticket I was once again mixing with the riff-raff (Trevor and Dave) on the terraces. Ian and Steve are still season ticket holders so I join Dave and Trevor in the South Bank as we watched 4-0 and 5-2 wins over Birmingham City and Coventry City respectively. You would think I would know better by now as things were destined to go the shape of a pear. Only one victory in the final twelve league games and yet we still manage to finish in ninth place. The F.A. cup would provide some optimism, in fact I'm so confident this is going to be our year that I've already gone out and been measured for my suit. Third round and its Wigan at home but the 1-0 win comes at a cost. Alan Devonshire is badly hurt with an ankle ligament injury and he will be out of action for quite some time. This was a massive blow to us as it was a beautiful sight to see Dev in full flow. He would often drop deep and Phil Parkes would roll the ball out to him and he would be off, I swear that man could catch pigeons. His close control was excellent and watching him link up with Trevor Brooking was a sight to behold. Without Dev, getting to Wembley just got a whole lot more difficult.

The famous five went to Crystal Palace for round four where a late Dave Swindlehurst goal earns us another bite at the cherry securing a 1-1 draw. We are all available for the replay (I'm determined not to send the suit back). A 2-0 win and I tell Marie don't book any holidays for May I reckon I might be busy. The next round requires us to travel up the motorway to Birmingham as the dream lives on. The famous five are all fired up for this one. It was all so different in those days, someone would say who fancies going to Luton, Southampton or wherever and off we'd go. Not like today where points need to be collected in order to purchase a ticket in advance, all we had to do was to pay on the day. So we are off to Birmingham and we get a bit lost at spaghetti junction, it's called this as they made a right bollocknese of it. The situation calls for some assistance via some local knowledge, so Ian opens his window to speak to some bloke asking "How do you get to St. Andrews?" The local comes back with "my brother takes me". I think that must be an example of the famous brummie 'shining wit' and yes that spoonerism was intended.

Eventually we arrive at the ground where the West Ham support is once more admirable. Our section is behind the goal and we make our way in, but before the game starts we consider it a good idea to go and 'splash our boots'. They have outside toilets here; I knew we should have put our watches back ten years before coming to this place. Anyway we take up our position to find we only have some flimsy piece of netting separating us from their fans. The game is not fifteen minutes old and already we are 2-0 down. Now these loveable brummies have a quaint custom to welcome their guests as they began to pelt us with missiles, darts and coins. Now I was seriously thinking about picking up a 50p, 20p, and 10p coin and throwing them back with a dart and shouting "one scum dead and eighty!" It was only a thought and no I didn't do it. The coins continued to shower down on us, if this is what it is like when they are winning I hate to think what happens when they are losing. The situation gets worse and there is a pitch invasion by the West Ham fans. Unfortunately the West Ham players don't invade the Birmingham penalty area and we go down 3-0. Oh well, I bet the suit wouldn't have fitted me properly anyway.

Trevor was irate; in fact I had not seen him this angry since our holiday in Jersey. What led to his anger then was when Trevor, Steve and I went into St. Helier. They had a maze which was constructed of two-way glass, thus enabling people outside to watch those trying to get out. There was also a tannoy system relaying the merry laughter of those unable to locate the exit. Anyway, Steve and I got out assuming Trevor was right behind us only he wasn't. From outside we watched his struggle and he was getting more and more frustrated. It reached a point where over the tannoy could be heard the sound of "come back you bastards, and how the f... do I get out of here?" Passers-by were looking up in amazement until eventually a small boy led him out. I'm positive Trevor won't thank me for relating that story but it had to be told.

The season ended with us 'potless' again but there were some highlights, one of the best being the 4-1 home win over spurs. Steve and Ian were in their seats and Dave and I were in the North Bank for this one. During this match Ray Stewart hit a fabulous volley from way out which still ranks as my favourite of all of his goals. Hopefully it won't be too long before Dev returns as we sure do miss him. Of the last nine games we fail to score in six of them.

# **Thanks Trev**

At this point in my life I was not getting to go to many of the games with the boys. There would still be the odd Friday night at Sweeneys for a glass of the 'falling down water' and a catch up with the lads, Steve's favourite drink was the next one. We now have a daughter, and with all the extra things needed space is at a premium. I then make the difficult decision to sell my collection of hammers programmes. There was an advert in the paper stating programmes bought along with a name and number to call. So I phoned the guy and he asked which team I collected, how many did I have and were they complete season's of home and away issues. Following a pleasant chat he informed me of his interest and said he would visit the next weekend as he was travelling from London. On arrival he checked a few to determine the condition and said he would be happy to take the lot. In hindsight I wished now that I had hung on to a few of the more special ones such as the cup finals testimonials and my first visit. It was a sad day when they went but needs must.

Among the few games I did get to a couple stand out, one of which was a tasty 3-1 win over the 'gooners'. The other was when the famous five went to Plough Lane to see the F.A. cup tie against Wimbledon. Plough Lane was an all seater stadium-they had a three piece suite behind each goal! As usual we are behind the goal and the steps had more or less eroded away. Before the game it had been raining and it was just like standing on the side of a hill. We were forever sliding down as we could not keep our footing. The game ended all square 1-1 with the highlight being the inclusion of Dev back in the starting line up. It was to be a long haul back for him as he would only make one more appearance that season. In my humble opinion I think had he not got injured and been out for so long, I don't believe Trevor Brooking would have retired when he did. The pair were a fantastic partnership and I sensed that Brooking did miss him. We all went to Brooking's last game in the claret and blue, plus on this occasion Steve's dad Dave is with us. When Steve and I were growing up he was very good to me and made me so welcome in his home. I had a lot of respect for the man and it was always interesting to listen to his 'back in the day' stories. He would tell tales of his favourite players, the likes of Len Goulden, Kenny Tucker and Joe Foxall. We are playing Everton and the scene was set for us to send Trevor off with one last hurrah. All we have to do is play eye-catching football and score a hat full of goals in a handsome victory; the only problem is Everton haven't read the memo. The evening was emotional, the result predictable as we get beat 1-0. All in all the fans said good bye and thank you to Trevor in style.

Our local paper The Evening Echo ran a competition about Trevor Brooking. There were eight questions about the man himself to be answered and for the tie breaker you had to write in twenty five words or less why you admired him. I knew the answers to all eight questions so figured it must be worth a shot at the tie breaker. My entry was as follows; dedication, professionalism, sportsmanship and outstanding ability are his main characteristics. A true ambassador for football, to inspire all ages. His talent will be missed worldwide.  The following week when reading through a copy of the Evening Echo I happened upon the result and was astonished to see that I had won. The prize was an all expenses paid trip to Sandown races for the Coral Eclipse day. Marie and I had a fantastic day beginning on the Saturday morning when a car came to collect us and we were chauffeur driven to the track. Upon arrival we were told we could have anything we wanted to drink from soft drinks to champagne. Normally the wine I drink is a cross between Muscatel and Hock (called muck). A three course lunch and afternoon tea were included plus money to bet with. The Corals representative informed us we were allowed to watch the races from any vantage point we saw fit. For one race I went out on to the television gantry and stood by the commentators. Nowhere was off limits to us, as we went in to the parade ring to chat with the jockeys. We ate in the Coral suite where some of our fellow diners were Mick Mills (Ipswich and England), Andy Lloyd (England and Warwickshire batsman), Peter o' Sullivan (racing commentator), Bobby George (darts player) and so many others. In fact there were so many famous people there I was the only one I'd never heard of.

Bobby George was the most sociable of all of the celebs. Marie had gone to the ladies and I was on my own, that was until Bobby (he lets me call him that now) came over and said "on your own then?" I explained that I had won a competition and that Marie had gone to 'powder her nose'. During our conversation he put me at my ease and said that if we were on our own and had nobody to talk to, just join him at his table and we would be most welcome. He asked what I had to do to win the competition and when I said it was about Trevor Brooking we had found common ground. Speaking with great affection he went on to talk about Manor Park and the East end and I felt relaxed in his company. At the time Corals were sponsoring him and it was in his contract to attend a certain number of their functions. A polite and friendly man and it was my pleasure to have met him. We used our betting money wisely and came away fourty pounds to the good.

Mum and Dad came on holiday with Marie and I and we went to Norfolk to Potters Leisure Resort. The food there is excellent (5,000 flies can't all be wrong). Just my little joke, the food was good. At breakfast on the Monday morning it was announced that anyone who fancied a kick-about should be on the football pitch at ten thirty, so that was my morning taken care of. When I got to the pitch the person in charge of this game was none other than Martin Peters. He told us that every Friday afternoon there was a match between the staff and the guests, and today he was going to sort out a team to go up against them. Practice complete the team is picked and I'm in so roll on Friday. On the afternoon of the game one of our team fails to show leaving us with ten men. It had to be done, we persuade Martin Peters to play on our side. Now the staff play this fixture every week and have a settled side, whereas we are a team of total strangers 'cobbled together' for this one off affair. I managed to score one but it's now well into the second half and we are losing 3-2. Martin Peters plays a one-two with me and I tuck it away for a 3-3 draw. Now I realise Martin Peters had a great understanding with Geoff Hurst but just for a minute there.................... After the game was over I tried to talk him into signing for Fryerns but he said he was too busy (very diplomatic)

# It's Goodnight from Me

It was July 1987 and to say my life was stressful would be something of an understatement. I was working for Her Majesty's Stationery Office, along with my dad who was also employed there and we were in the process of relocating. My duties within the company would also be changing. Marie was five months pregnant with our second child, and we were in the middle of moving home as we needed a larger house for our growing family.

If that wasn't enough to cope with it was to get a whole lot worse. It was the week before sixteen of us were due to go on the family holiday to Norfolk, and my dad and I had arranged to have a game of tennis when we had finished work on the Friday afternoon. So there we were in the middle of our game when tragedy struck as from out of nowhere he suffered a massive heart attack and died. The man who had protected me under his coat all those years ago and who had continued to look out for me in each and every one of the years that followed had died. And so had my love for playing football only it would be a little later before I would realise this. I had just lost my tennis mate, my workmate, my football mate and my best mate. I went with him in the ambulance to the hospital, and when we got there was immediately asked to wait in a side room. A police officer entered to explain that I had to complete some paperwork and that they would go through it with me. I was still in a state of shock as dad had always been such a fit man. It's strange how certain pieces of information stay with you forever, one such piece being that officer's name and I've no idea why I can still remember it to this day. It was W.P.C. Corbett who helped me with the paper work. When it was completed it suddenly dawned on me I still had to tell my mum. What's the worst job you've ever had? W.P.C. Corbett offered to drive me to mum's house saying she would come in if I wanted her to, or wait in the car for a while until she knew we were both o.k. This officer had shown me nothing but kindness and compassion throughout my ordeal, only I was so engulfed in my own grief I never took the time to thank her. W.P.C. Corbett please accept a very belated thank you.

I had chosen not to speak at dad's funeral, not because I didn't want to, but because I did not think I would be strong enough. This choice would turn out to be the correct one. On cup final days when Abide with Me was sung dad would get emotional and say how that always gave him goose bumps so it was only natural mum and I wanted this to be the first song at his funeral. Well I stood up to sing, opened my mouth but nothing came out. Instead I just stood there remembering being at West Ham's cup finals in 1975 and 1980 and us standing side by side, shoulder to shoulder with him, singing Abide with Me on a day when the words did come out.

I signed on for another season with Fryerns F.C. which began in September but playing would never be the same again for me. After all of those Saturdays and Sundays with him on the touchline it was weird with him not being there. Don't get me wrong he didn't come along just to massage my ego, regardless of my performance be it good bad or indifferent he would always let me know I can assure you. He was so happy just to watch me play and all I ever wanted to do was to make him proud. You may say professional players lose a loved one but continue to play, but that it what they are paid to do in order to provide for their family. In my case I was paid to work in a factory to provide for my family and continued to do so. The difference being that for me football was a pleasure, and that pleasure was no longer there for me. I played a couple of more games and decided to call it a day.

Creators of the author

Kingswood Junior School Under 11's

Cup winners Bela United
Steve Lloyd holds aloft the trophy, front row
second from right is me, third from right is Billy
Bingham

Me proudly
displaying the rug
I got for my
eighteenth
birthday

Pemberry Athletic Front R to L, Billy Bingham, Me, Steve Lloyd

E.S.L. League Champions
Front row extreme right is me, third from right holding the trophy is my dad
Back row second from left Steve Lloyd, third from left Billy Bingham, eight from left is Johnny Martin

Terry Venables gets the chance to meet me

From left to right Me, Trevor, Steve and Derek on
holiday in Jersey

Outside the Heysel Stadium in Brussels
From right to left Dave, Trevor, Sparrer, Me, A. N.
Other and Steve

Bowers United Reserve side who beat Basildon 2—0 in Tuesday evening's derby at Gardiners Lane

Front row second from right is me, extreme left is
Billy Bingham

Fryerns F.C.
I'm front row extreme right

Marie and
me about to
go out to
dinner to
celebrate
our
engagement

Dave Foulgar, of Codenham Straight, Basildon, was married to Marie Cole, of Roodegate, Basildon, at Holy Cross Church, Basildon. Photo: Ray Panter

From left to right Steve, me and Dave at a party at Steve's parents house

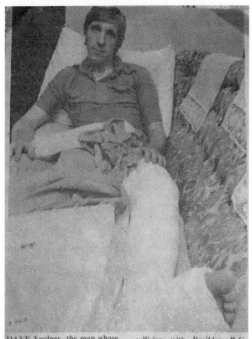

DAVE Foulger, the man whose tremendous goalscoring feats have rocketed Basildon Town to the top of the Southend and District League Premier Division, will be out of action for the rest of the season.

Foulger broke his left leg in a collision with Basildon B.C. defender Roger Gorbell as Town slipped to a 2—0 defeat — their first loss of the season.

And Foulger, who had scored 22 goals before Saturday, was playing his 13th game for Town.

From left to right Trevor, Me and Dave at Steve and Viv's wedding

Second from right Dave, I'm fourth from right then
Viv, Ian and Trevor

League Champions Fryerns
I'm front row third from right

Thank you West Ham for allowing me this moment

What the well dressed man is wearing about town these days

DAVE and Marie Foulger, from Basildon, are pictured with Mrs Sue Sangster (right) after the Coral Eclipse race at Sandown Park on Saturday.

The Foulgers, winners of the Coral / Echo Trevor Brooking competition, were congratulating Sue, wife of the owner of the winning horse Sadler's Wells.

It was a great day out for the Foulgers, who were special guests of Coral. They were wined and dined and had a chance to meet the owners and jockeys in the unsaddling enclosure.

And, with their betting vouchers, they came out winning £40. "Watching racing on television is never going to be the same again after this," said Dave, as he sipped champagne in the scorching sun.

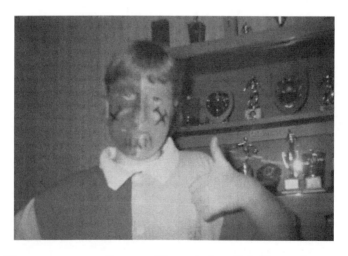

Even at an early age I'm giving Melissa tips on how to do her make-up

It has
been
my
good
fortune
to have
known
Steve

Marie, Me,
Viv and
Steve
enjoying a
new years
eve party

When they had learnt the words to bubbles Melissa
and Martin were allowed back in the house

Martin relaxing and showing how a bedroom
should be decorated

Julian Dicks agrees to be my minder

Melissa and Martin are also proud to wear the claret and blue alongside me

Our pride and joy

Marie

Thank you for being a wonderful wife and mother

# **Moving On**

Marie gave birth to our second chid and we have a son to make our family complete, a boy and a girl. Long ago I had imagined that if ever I was lucky enough to have a son I would like to name him after whoever was captain of West Ham at that time. Well when our son came along skippering the hammers was Alvin Martin. I had always been a great fan of 'stretch' and admired his contribution to our cause, but I couldn't bring myself to name our boy Alvin. What we did was to take the next option and our son was named Martin. Our captain would not be forgotten as Melissa was reaching the age where she was interested in having a pet; a trip to the local pet shop was called for as she had her heart set on a goldfish. When the assistant approached us I asked him if we could have a goldfish to which he responded "do you want an aquarium?" To which I replied "I don't care what star sign it is". So Melissa ended up with two goldfish and named them Alvin and Martin.

At this stage in the proceedings Dave, Steve, Ian and I were all married men with our own families and Trevor was spoken for. We all had responsibilities and before you know it we are not seeing as much of each other as we used to. There were no rows or arguments we were all just getting on with living our own lives. From a personal point of view I wished that I had made more of an effort to keep in touch but life gets in the way.

We have got two children and we are struggling to buy our own home so I was hardly going to Upton Park at all. At first the interest rate wasn't too bad then before we know it we are up to 15%, and things are so bad I can't even afford to pay attention. This was Maggie Thatcher's master plan to give you the chance to buy your own home and then whack up the interest rate. I think she even gave long term prisoners the chance to buy their own cell! I was still making sure that the kids had plenty of food on the table, and plenty of claret and blue in the wardrobe. One of my favourites was a t- shirt that Melissa had and printed on the front of it was the slogan I SUPPORT WEST HAM COS MY DAD SAYS SO. Naturally this was passed down to Martin.

Our neighbourhood community centre had begun to organise a mother and toddler group. The mums would meet a couple of times a week for a coffee and a chat while the children played. As well as the children making new friends it was also a good opportunity for the mums to do likewise. Whilst chatting to one of the other mums Marie was explaining how fanatical I was about West Ham. She then said that she had one just like me at home and that we should get together. This was planned and that is how I came to meet fellow hammer Paul Manning. We instantly struck up a rapport became friends and went to a few games together. Walthamstow dog track was the scene for one of Ray Stewart's testimonial functions and Paul got us tickets for the event. An enjoyable meal was followed by an evening of greyhound racing and an auction of West Ham memorabilia. We never bought anything, and more to the point we never bid for anything, the prices were well out of our league. At least we did get to meet Ray and have a chat and I also had the privilege of meeting Leroy Rosenior, what a nice guy he was. Both were happy to have a photo taken with me, it's just a pity the dogs never ran like they were supposed to.

I am still working at Her Majesty's Stationery Office and we have a new recruit joining our ranks. The most obvious questions to ask when a new guy starts are what's your name and where do you come from (sorry Cilla). Well not in our department it isn't, our leading question is "who do you support". The new starter is a West Ham fan who I then find out is Phil Parmenter. We went on to become firm friends and Phil's wife Debbie got on with Marie and the four of us spent many a pleasant evening enjoying one another's company. When they came to visit us our children liked them and insisted they played some of their board games with them before bedtime. They would come to us for a meal and vice versa. It wasn't just a case of Phil and myself going to Upton Park, the four of us plus the children would go to Romford dogs or for days out. Phil and Debbie went on to have two children of their own. Yes, I know there's something about West Ham fans I always seem to get on with them and so far haven't met one that I didn't like.

West Ham have many various ways of testing our loyalty and what they served up for us this season was another one of their novel inventions. It was uninspiring; in the last fifteen games we fired blanks in ten of them. In previous seasons when we have gone down, right up until the final nail went into the coffin I always held the belief that we were good enough to escape the drop. This year however the writing was on the wall from a long way out. Going into work on a Monday morning preparing to face the barrage of abuse and knowing I was going to 'get it ripped out of me' was never a great way to start the working week. At least Phil was there to share my pain. It was Martin Godleman who said our days are few and how right he is, and 1991 can't end quickly enough for me.

On the plus side is that in the home programme versus Sheffield Wednesday there is a feature on me. The section is called Fan file and there is a photograph of me along with my answers to various questions. For example, best game ever, favourite all time player, first game ever seen etc. This is one edition I'm never going to part with. Having previously sold my extensive collection of programmes I am now keeping the ones from games I attend and other what I consider to be special programmes.

# Claret and Blues

Melissa continues to be my companion for pre-season friendlies with the promise of a visit to Upton Park to come. I tell her that if she keeps on misbehaving I will make her go and watch them. Paul asked me if I was interested in going to the away match at Arsenal to which I obviously agree. I am not quite ready to desert our sinking ship; I'm a glutton for punishment. Even though it's in London we travel by coach with the other hammers faithful. To be honest I was going more in hope than expectation as you just never know with our boys, after all we are now into November and we have only tasted victory on four occasions. You don't need Mystic Meg to tell me what kind of year this will develop into.

We are by the corner flag next to the clock end trying not to wake up the librarians. The lads have chosen today to treat us to one of their better displays, and a 'cracker' from the edge of the box by Mike Small gives us a most welcome 1-0 win. This wasn't shown on Match of the Day but did feature on Tales of the Unexpected! Although I never went to a huge amount of games with Paul I can only ever remember seeing us lose once. That's where you are going wrong West Ham; you should have made sure that he went to every game. The 'drop' is looming and we need to sign Stephen Hendry as we are so far behind on points we now need snookers.

Guidelines laid out in the Taylor Report stipulate that all top flight grounds must be converted into all seated stadiums. West Ham come up with 'a cunning plan' to try to ensure that it will be the fans who foot the bill. For a minimum payout of five hundred pounds you then had the opportunity to purchase a season ticket. Yeah right, good luck with that one at least Dick Turpin wore a mask. The board who do not know shit from strawberries have seriously misjudged the level of unrest amongst the claret and blue army. The ensuing protests have the desired effect and the board are forced to pull the plug on this ill-conceived scheme, and the day has been won. Us hammers fans have been known to follow our club with a blind passion but there comes a time when you have to stand up and be counted and say enough is enough.

One game I did miss out on was the F.A. cup semi-final against Nottingham Forest at Villa Park, oh how I wished I could have been there. The game was live on the box and Marie had taken the children to visit her brother and I was Macaulay

Culkin (home alone). When referee Keith Hackett wrongly dismissed Tony Gale mid way through the first half our chances were reduced to slim. Even so, we managed to hit the woodwork but there was only ever going to be one winner once we are playing with a man down. It was questionable if Gale had fouled their player Crosby at all, but to compound matters it wasn't a goal scoring opportunity as he was running away from the goal, and Gale wasn't the last defender. This referee was proof that Snow White and Dopey did have sex!

In the face of adversity the thing that amazed me most was those fantastic fans. The chant of 'Billy Bonds claret and blue army' reverberated around the ground continuously for around twenty five minutes. What I would have given to have been a part of that choir, they were unbelievable. At the moment Marie arrived home we were losing 3-0. She walked in and hearing the chanting remarked "that sounds good how many are you winning by?" She was astonished when I told her we were getting beat 3-0. On my next visit to Upton Park I bought a t-shirt which had printed on it about thirty times BILLY BONDS CLARET AND BLUE ARMY which I proudly wore to many a game.

Paul and I went to the Charlton away fixture and he said this time he was going to drive. His chosen route was via the Woolwich Ferry, I think this was because he wanted to stock up on the duty free. It was Charlton we were playing but they were ground sharing with Crystal Palace so Selhurst Park was our destination. When the fans were chanting 'Billy Bonds claret and blue army' at the cup semi final Paul had recorded it from the radio commentary on to cassette tape. So on our way to Selhurst Park we had this to listen to, miles better than any radio station or pop c.d. During this period we were being sponsored by the window company B.A.C. the inspired chant we would sing was 'B.A.C. means back as champions'. This was because we were about to leave division two, ready to dine at the top table of division one. We most definitely jinxed that one. O.K. so we did win promotion but not as the champions that we should have been. A home defeat on the last day of the season left us in runners-up position thus handing the title to Oldham. Promotion was great but when you are within touching distance of winning the title and having a trophy, to finally come second does tend to somewhat take the gloss off of the achievement.

# Win Some, Win Some More

After being lucky enough to win the prize of a day at the races I was now entering many more competitions. These would be in various newspapers and on radio stations and my luck was continuing to hold. The majority of my wins came via Radio 5 and in particular Dominik Diamonds shows called Sportscall and Newscall and the rewards were excellent. I was fortunate to win lots of sports memorabilia, books and match day tickets. Essex radio was another station where I met with considerable success.

A new football craze was starting to take off and this was known as Fantasy Football. This involved selecting a team made up of premier league players and how well they performed for their teams earned you points. For example defenders would score five points for a clean sheet, goals scored would earn five points and assists had a value of two points. More than one goal conceded by a defender and you enter the territory of minus points. Each player had a fictional value and spending was restricted to a pre determined budget. B.B.C. radio 5 live devoted a one and a half hour programme to this every week. We organised leagues at work and would play against other managers across the country. In 1992 my fantasy team exceeded my expectations and I became National champion, and helped Paul to set up a league for him and his workmates. By this time the B.B.C. had latched on to this format and produced a weekly show called Fantasy Football League starring Frank Skinner and David Baddiel. The guys who worked in the offices of the original Fantasy Football kindly sent me four tickets to go and see the show being recorded. I gave a ticket each to Phil Parmenter, John Sussex and Paul Wood. We had to make our way to the Avalon studios which were located in Wandsworth, and John Sussex was to be our designated driver.

It was permitted to wear club colours and as we entered we were given free beer which we were then allowed to take in with us. This would be totally different to what I expected to happen at a T.V. show recording. There were no men holding up signs saying 'clap now' or 'laugh'. The floor manager told us that the camera would roll for approximately two hours, and later the best bits would be edited for the half hour show that would go out on the Friday evening. Skinner and Baddiel were on great form that night and we certainly didn't need to be prompted to laugh. The two guest managers in the studio were Patsy Kensit and Nick

Hornby plus of course Statto and Jeff Astle. I assume that it must have been a quite thankless task trying to edit it into thirty minutes as there was so much good material. At the finish they did not just say good night and leave, they stayed and made themselves available to audience members who wanted to chat. Never one to look a gift horse in the mouth I went to exchange a few words; the verdict was a thoroughly entertaining evening. We got to see ourselves on television on the Friday night show but I still never received that B.A.F.T.A. My fantasy team that won me the national title was named after my Sunday league side consisting of mainly West Ham fans it was called E.S.L. Irons. Explaining how much fun I was getting from playing Fantasy Football Ian expressed an interest and was keen to become involved. One afternoon I met up with Ian and several of his workmates and helped to organise a league for their own company. This was addictive, and it wasn't too long before the national newspapers got hold of the format and instead of winning trophies large cash prizes were to be found at the end of the rainbow.

Martin's bedroom needed decorating and so the West Ham wallpaper was going up (the value of our property is definitely going up). He needed new fitted wardrobes so we called someone in to do the job. The guy noticed the hammers items all around the place and informed me that he was doing some work at the home of one of the players. This turned out to be our mid field player Peter Butler. I suppose my initial reply should have been something along the lines of "where does he live" or "is it a large house" or maybe even "what sort of work are you doing for him". But no not me, being the mercenary that I am I went straight for the obvious "any chance you can get me some tickets?" Being a bit cheeky paid dividends as he came up with two seats in the West Stand for the encounter with Swindon Town. The lucky recipient of one free ticket was to be Paul Manning; who was it said there's no such thing as a free lunch. The match itself was a big let down as George Parris gets himself sent off and we don't perform in a 1-0 defeat. I remember remarking to Paul "this could have been a whole lot worse", and his response was "how do you make that out?" I then said "we could have paid for these tickets".

In the F.A. cup we had drawn 0-0 against non league Farnborough Town (it still sounds as bad now I'm writing it as when I watched it!) Expecting an avalanche of goals in the replay Paul and I have half a mind to go, and the way we are playing that's about all you need to watch them. For this one we have treated ourselves to seats in the East Stand and are mightily relieved to see Trevor Morley spare our blushes with a last minute winner, (I saw a fat lady clearing her throat). In adversity hammers fans can still come out with some little gems. During the game the Farnborough winger goes down the line and floats over a cross which Ludo comes off his line and claims comfortably. Farnborough players had all pushed up and Morley was making a run to the halfway line unmarked, screaming for Ludo to release the ball early. With that Ludo promptly drop kicked the ball, only to slice it badly straight into the chicken run. He then held up his arm in acknowledgement to Morley. It was at this moment a fan seated behind me shouted "you don't have to put your hand up, we saw who done it".

The next round was Wrexham away and Paul invited me to his home to watch the game on television, another 1-0 win and the dream lives on. Round five and yet another away tie this time at Sunderland. A creditable 1-1 result brings them back to our place and surely the hard work is done. But what you have to remember is this is West Ham we are talking about. A 3-2 defeat and the dream is over for another year. To rub salt into the wound for Phil Parmenter he went to the game only to be locked out, (that'll teach him to forget his key).

# **Premium Bonds**

The ritual of going to pre season friendlies continues as Melissa comes with me and I promise her that this year I will take her to a league match at Upton Park. Meanwhile we go to Southend for the friendly game and stop to watch the street entertainers, one of which was a mime artist. A policeman deemed him to be causing an obstruction and wanted him to move along. He declined this offer and proceeded to carry on with his act ignoring the officer's instructions. Not having been able to convince the mime artist to move on the policeman felt he was left with no other alternative and was trying to arrest the mime artist when he came out with what I thought to be a classic line "are you going to come quietly?" (Well it made me laugh anyway).

Due to some special promotion my mum is now getting Sky T.V. free for six months and tells me that when the hammers are on both Phil and I are more than welcome to go round and watch. Needless to say we didn't need to be asked twice. Bonzo was now the manager and had got the team playing well and the season would end with only two home defeats and fifty goals scored. Clive

Allen and Trevor Morley had formed a formidable partnership up front.

Great player that Billy Bonds was, he was never one that I would have earmarked as manager material. Not that I had doubts regarding his capabilities, it was more due to the fact that he loved his home life. Many times I have read that when the game was over Bill would be the first one changed and back home to his family. The down side of being a manager is that it tends to take you away from your family even more so than when you are a player. Going out in mid week to run the rule over a potential signing, or to spy on the future opposition. Also I would imagine there would be a considerable amount of office time dealing with players and agents and this prolonging the working day leaving even less quality time with his family. I'm glad he did become our boss because he never suffered fools gladly and understood us fans and how we hoped to see our team play. Therefore I guess he had sacrificed a lot of his personal life to try to give us the team we wanted. The final game of the season pairs us with Cambridge United at home. A win is vital if promotion is to be achieved. Four of us are going Paul, Phil, Melissa and me. Melissa was thrilled to be going and a full house added to a terrific atmosphere. Already 1-0 in front and not too long to go Julian Dicks goes on a surging run down the left wing. He wins a tackle and lays it on a plate for Clive Allen to tap home for goal number two and the place goes wild. At the final whistle jubilant fans covered the pitch; sadly, this didn't include us as we were in the West side upper tier and even after a couple of 'lemonades' the jump down appeared to be beyond us. We were promoted job done and Melissa said she was more than happy to come again. It's experiencing good times like this that can go a long way to cementing a bond for our younger fans to keep the faith.

Mum is getting a right result with Sky as the free trial period has expired but she is still able to view the games. Phil and I have season tickets for the sofa and are ever presents when the hammers are on. With the F.A. cup semi finals taking place at Wembley once again we are within touching distance. A quarter final draw sends Luton Town our way and Phil and I are glued to the screen. It's a scrappy 0-0 draw but we get to see another game on the box. At their place with the scores level at 2-2 Steve Potts miss controls the ball on the half way line and they break away to net the winner. We would have been 'certs' for the final as it was only Chelsea waiting in the semi final.

A pattern was beginning to develop here as Phil and I turned up at mum's for our away game at Sheffield United. From cruising to go 2-0 up (well maybe not cruising but paddling really hard) we go on to lose 3-2. Billy Bonds stops all the players from owning a dog and says it is because they can't hang on to a lead. Why is it that West Ham have to get four goals in front before I am relaxed and comfortable, and then I'm still not sure?

The final game of the season sends Southampton our way and I am taking Melissa to spend some quality time with West Ham. I have won another competition this time on Capital Gold radio and have two seats in the Bobby Moore Upper tier. To make the day extra special for me the opposition have one of the players that I have always admired-Matt le Tissier. I suppose it would be fair comment to say that he was so laid back he thought Valium was a stimulant. He was one of the few players, who could put weight ON in ninety minutes, but the guy was so talented and almost every goal he scored was a 'worldie'. A great game ended in a 3-3 draw and Le Tiss netted twice (I did warn you West Ham but you don't listen to me).

Back in the day nearly every team had one entertainer similar to Le Tiss who fans would go along to watch. For instance Manchester United had George Best, Q.P.R. had Stan Bowles, Sheffield United had Tony Currie, Leeds United had Eddie Gray, and Frank Worthington played for, well you can take your pick. But another who I liked was Alan Hudson of Chelsea, now he could really pass a ball (if only he could have passed a pub). Of course I wanted us to win every game but I could still appreciate a bit of skill displayed by an opposing player even if it did hurt. To be honest I must admit I was more appreciative of their skill if it was just a consolation goal as we were 3-0 up at the time. There are times when you have to give someone credit for displaying some degree of skill, rather than always looking to blame one of our own.

# Martin Makes His Debut

Down at the Boleyn it is all change as Harry Redknapp takes over from Billy Bonds. There were to be many conflicting reports regarding the breakdown of the working relationship between the two, I seriously wonder if we will ever learn the truth. To this day the pair still do not speak to one another.

It is difficult to keep up with the new arrivals and the departures as Harry certainly likes to do a deal. I reckon the player's dressing room doesn't have a door, more likely a turnstile. On Dominik Diamond's Sportscall radio programme he is giving away tickets for West Ham versus Crystal Palace. Phil Parmenter is glad that I've entered this competition because I have won and chose to give him the other ticket. This time we are in the West Enclosure and I have not been in this part of the stadium since they put seats here. It's a strange feeling sitting here by the tunnel remembering all those years ago when I stood there collecting autographs. The prize includes hospitality and we take full advantage as we don't like to offend. A game that wasn't the greatest I'd ever witnessed had the points sealed for us by a Don Hutchison header.

As I am on a hot streak with regard to the competitions I am now even entering non football related ones. The next prize to come my way is a weekend away at the world water skiing championships (how did they manage to find a lake with a slope?). They were held at a resort in Reading and the hotel was brilliant. An old mate called Phil Finch came with me and we had a good time as the hotel provided a swimming pool, tennis courts, casino plus other amenities. We sat down for our Sunday lunch and on the next table were seated several cast members from the television show Emmerdale. Phil was, and still is a spurs fan (the medication hasn't kicked in yet) so it was a real education for him to encounter electric lights, carpet etc.

I give Martin his Upton Park debut and take him to the Leicester City game. Dull it isn't as Don Hutchison is sent off and Julian Dicks smashes home one of his trademark penalties. Martin and I are seated in the Bobby Moore stand and are right behind the thunderbolt of a spot kick. It was pleasing to record a welcome home win for Martin's first visit. At least Harry had the good sense to bring Julian back home; those scousers didn't appreciate a good thing when they had him. They probably weren't too happy that they had to pay decent money for him. Preferring to get him on the cheap so then they can say in true scouse fashion 'they stole him'.

Tony Cottee comes back to where he belongs and Harry has managed to turn things around. Marc Reiper has tightened things up at the back and in the last nine league games we only let in four goals. There's a sentence I never dreamed that I'd be writing.

The first game of season 1995/96 is at home to Leeds United and we are greeted with a beautiful sunny day. There are four of us walking down Green Street full of excitement and anticipation for the coming campaign. The four in question are Phil Parmenter, Melissa, Martin and I. Today we are in the upper tier of the Trevor Brooking stand, the family area. It only takes five minutes for Danny Williamson to put us in front, a lead which we keep until half time. Two Leeds goals bring us back down to earth and already we are on page two of the teletext league table. Marco Boogers comes on in the second half and is a player of whom I know very little. He took up a position out wide on the right. His first involvement was when a ball was played to his feet, with plenty of pitch in front of him to exploit. I'm sure like me many were waiting for him to burst down the wing. Instead, under no pressure whatsoever he knocks the ball about ten yards in front of him, straight into touch. Yeah don't set the bar too high Marco. The next game away at Manchester United he almost cuts Gary Neville in half with a late tackle (he got there as soon as he could) and gets sent off. Rumour had it that he went back to Holland to live in a caravan and suffered with mental health issues.

Sky T.V. have now realised the error of their ways and my mum can no longer get the football on her television causing Phil and myself no little heartache. Phil and Debbie are now married and buy a house that is about a ten minute walk from ours. Sky TV. is installed and I am invited whenever the hammers are on the box which I am extremely grateful for. At the same time my next door neighbour Roy has Sky and I'm spoilt for invitations. This situation is handy for me as I have been made redundant from my job and as I am not going too frequently 'all donations' are gratefully received'.

The reason for my redundancy is because Her Majesty's Stationery Office has chosen to relocate to London, The Elephant and Castle to be exact. The company wish for us all to make the move with them but the fly in the ointment is the prospect of new terms and conditions in our contract. This would involve shift work (I'm already a shift worker, anyone mentions work and I shift). The subsequent schedule of hours was not practical and because of the distance in extra travel redundancy was offered. I will more than likely end up being a wringer-out for a one armed window cleaner. A trip to the Unemployment Benefit Office was called for and i duly turned up for my interview. I was greeted by a lady and one of the first questions that she asked me was how much money I had in the bank. My instant reply was £150,000, and her response was "you're joking" to which I replied "you started it".

As welcome as T.V. viewing is I cannot go completely 'cold turkey' and stay away from Upton Park. Money wise things are tight (so bad I'm now selling pegs to the gypsies), but I can manage to take the children to three games. The financial implication was that I heard myself saying to Marie "how do you want your housekeeping this week, heads or tails" (and she just left me laying there).

Two of the games that we chose to attend would illustrate the highs and lows of late goals. Against Queens Park Rangers when in conversation with Phil the old cliché was trotted out-this one's got 0-0 written all over it, when close to full time Cottee does what he does best and 1-0 it is. The reverse of this scenario occurred in the fixture against Blackburn Rovers. Iain Dowie's goal appears to be good enough for three points today and we are out of our seats ready to leave as Alan Shearer equalises.

I take Melissa and Martin to the third round F.A. cup tie for the visit of Southend United, our good friend Phil Parmenter is part of our crew (yeah I'm down with the kids). They still enjoy going with me which in turn makes me feel good. As my dad did with me, I suppose I was choosing their team for them, and was just hoping that the day would never arrive when they would turn around and tell me they wanted to choose their own team. Thankfully that day has never arrived. So we beat Southend 2-0 and go out to Grimsby Town in the next round and our cup run is over. I say run, it was more of a jog. The only other game we take in is when Manchester City come calling. The fare on offer that day was the kind to keep the children begging me to take them back to sample more of the delights on our footballing menu. We play well and I am fully aware that simple fact doesn't mean that you are always going to win. But today our four goals trump their two. Throw into the mix Ludo saving a spot-kick, a Dicks'y special from twenty five yards and I would suggest that was better than spending the afternoon pushing the trolley round Tescos. There was also a fine individual goal by Dani. I say Dani; I think it was him only it might have been Iain Dowie because I always get those two mixed up as they look so alike! That's one for the real hammers fan's. This game would attract a full house and so the police were there in large numbers. It appears the way we are playing even they can't wait to see us in action. They bring with them not only their Alsatians but also sniffer dogs. Outside Upton Park station a copper stops one bloke near me, and he is greeted with "my dog tells me you are on drugs". To which he replied " I'm on drugs? You're the one with the talking dog". I never did hang around long enough to see if he was invited to spend some time in one of Her Majesty's holiday camps.

# Too Close for Comfort

The redundancy factor plays a major role in my friendship with Phil Parmenter. We are no longer working together and Phil has acquired another position that has unsociable hours, he will be working permanent nights. Obviously this makes it difficult to arrange to meet socially. Hammers News magazine ensures that we don't lose touch completely. I would buy it one month and after reading it would then pass it on to Phil. The following month Phil would buy it and then deliver it to me. When work allowed he would still invite me round for the television games. We try to find time for the odd night out and Romford Greyhound track is a popular venue for us. When I say us, that would include our wives and the children. Melissa and Martin were struggling to understand why the winner of every race was always called 'lucky bastard'.

By this time both Melissa and Martin were members of the Junior Hammers Club. This would entail a change to our match day routine as we would now leave earlier to spend some time in the club house. The children would have their faces painted, perhaps a game of table tennis, pool or even table football. We had something to eat and drink and watch some of the children joining in with some ball skill sessions. All part of the master plan to 'hook' our younger followers. When Melissa and Martin went to the games they loved to wear their replica shirts. On the back would be printed the name of their particular favourite player at the time. I can recall Melissa wearing shirts with Rio and Cole on. Martin had a shirt with Sinclair on, and on another he chose to have the name Dicks printed.

The programme for the league cup tie with Stockport County was a collector's item in our household as it featured a picture of Martin and Melissa plus a small write up. We are present to witness a 2-1 victory over Southampton with Julian Dicks lashing home a penalty in customary fashion. It was especially gratifying to see that one go in as the last time we had a 'biro' (sorry, pen) when I fetched the kids he missed it. That was against Arsenal and we got beat 1-0 on the day. It was not revealed until later that Julian was concussed when he took that one, the result of an earlier collision. He said he could never remember taking it and probably shouldn't have even been on the pitch. So yes, normal service has been resumed with the net bulging as expected after another Julian cannonball. Penalty taking really is an art and there are many different styles of executing the kick. Another plus factor is that you definitely need the right temperament. Therefore it is uncanny that our three best exponents Geoff Hurst, Ray Stewart and Julian Dicks all opted for the same method- power. Having said that, Mark Noble is certainly running them close in the 'reliability stakes'.

Our financial situation dictates that my visits will be far fewer this 1996 -97 season, but an opportunity presents itself. Martin has a birthday coming up and I ask him if he would like to invite a friend and we can go to a game as part of his birthday present. I breathe a sigh of relief as he agrees this is a good idea and promptly asks his friend Scott who is a Manchester United fan (well he does live in Essex). Previously in conversation with Phil I had told him of my plans for Martin's birthday, so I was delighted when he got back to me to let me know he had a free weekend and could come and the cherry on the cake was he would drive us there. Ian Bishop nets for us in a 1-1 draw, now seeing Ian Bishop score is much better than getting that new bike isn't it (oh it's just me then is it ?).

I may not be getting to see the players at Upton park much, but I am getting to see them in Basildon. Julian Dicks opened a sports shop in the town and Martin and I went along and got his autograph and had a photo of us all together, and we were to meet again in Basildon at his book signing (I'm not stalking you Julian, honestly). Melissa came with us to W.H. Smith to meet Tony Cottee when he was doing a book signing. He was very approachable and only too happy to oblige with autographs and photos. The big department store in the town was Alders and Alan Devonshire was there doing a meet and greet session to which we went along. Well it would have been rude not to.

As the season unfolds it would appear that I'm not missing out on too much after all. The quality of the football is questionable to say the least, and Harry's foreign legion doesn't seem to want to fight. Our season is going downhill faster than a rabbit on a promise. Harry convinces the board to let him go shopping and no not with Raducioiu. He brings in Paul Kitson and John Hartson and they breathe new life into the team, and me, but we are still drinking in the last chance saloon. I watch the home game versus spurs at Phil and Debbie's home, and it's a proper London derby played in awful conditions. Two goals from Julian plus one each from Kitson and Hartson and we are 4-3 winners and Sky T.V. subscribers have got their money's worth. It was one of the best games I had seen in ages, there was a passion displayed from West Ham that had gone walkabout for quite a while.

I am reminded of a similar situation back in 1976-77 when it seemed we were all but doomed (Captain Mainwaring). A Monday night home match against Manchester United and we have to win it as it is the last game of the season. For this one I am on my own due to the fact that I shall be going straight from work. As usual our support was tremendous, a crowd of almost 30,000 had squeezed into Upton Park and when I turned up the only part of the ground I could get into was the West Enclosure. Five minutes had elapsed and already we are one down and Pike would miss a penalty (stupid boy). I don't think I'm going to have enough fingernails left to last me ninety minutes. Pop Robson nets twice, Frank Lampard (the good one) scores, and Pike fires home a screamer, he's always been my favourite. The tension was there, the goals were there, and I was there. One of my favourite games at the Boleyn and when they play like that I can forgive them almost anything

That is why betting on West Ham is such a precarious business as you never know what you are likely to get. Quite often I will back against them so that we if we lose I win some money to cushion the blow. If I lose my money then I'm happy in the knowledge that we have three points and that's fine by me. It's when we draw that it begins to muddy the waters.

Hartson and Kitson plunder enough goals to keep us up after a mid season spell of one win in eighteen games when we are as about as good as a one legged man in an arse kicking contest! In actual fact there would only be three defeats in the final thirteen games which saved our rashers, though I must admit we did cut it fine. Being a West Ham fan should come with a government health warning. We are featured regularly on the television but it is not on Match of the Day, it's on that other programme-survival.

# It Must Be Love

Pre-season is upon us once again and our family along with Phil and Debbie's go to the family fun day at Upton Park. On a sunny day there are lots to do besides meeting some of the team, there were rides, games, competitions and souvenir stalls. As the weather has been kind to us the object of the exercise has been achieved. To capitalise on this we took a picnic and when we left the festivities we went to Valentines Park to enjoy our food and play with the kids. We had brought with us a football and a cricket set, good fun, good company and a thoroughly good day out.

Martin's tenth birthday was approaching and not wanting to disappoint him bought tickets for us to go to the Aston Villa match. Can you spot a pattern developing here? I was hoping this would be a worthwhile birthday treat as the quality of our play was as good as ever. But West Ham have caught me out like that before, they lure me into a false sense of security and then...... Having said that, they could have been on the crest of a slump and we would still have wanted to go. As previously mentioned when it comes to West Ham's form it's more often than not a case of 'you pays your money, you takes your chance'.

Now we have Trevor Sinclair, Eyal Berkovic, Steve Lomas and Ian Pearce in our ranks, and with Rio Ferdinand settling in well we ventured forth full of optimism. Prior to the game I had written to the programme editors sending a picture of Martin and a short write up about him. I had decided to keep this information from him, all the while secretly hoping for his inclusion in the match day edition. At Upton Park station I bought a programme and gave it to him with fingers crossed. When he turned over a page and was met with the sight of his photo his face was a picture. My efforts had not been in vain and someone up there was smiling down on me that day, providing another keepsake. To cap a most pleasurable birthday treat, two goal John Hartson sends us home all smiles and it's a case of 'winner winner, chicken dinner'. Our seats were up in the family area of the Trevor Brooking stand. Times like these make me thankful I can get us seats in order for Martin to experience a decent view. This is because he is still quite small for his age; in fact he is so small that on his passport photo you can see his feet.

A mid week league cup encounter against Walsall provides an opportunity to get 'another fix' and this time we are joined by Melissa. Unfortunately for us this time I can only get us seats in the lower tier of the Trevor Brooking stand. To be honest with the children in attendance this is not my favourite vantage point. I much prefer them to be higher up looking down to see more of the build up play. The view we had was more at ground level giving the impression the other goal was some way in the distance, or are West Ham trying to break me in gently in preparation for the move to Stratford. Anyway we are compensated for an 'iffy' view with a handsome 4-1 victory on the night. An evening out at the Boleyn on a school night whatever next, I don't remember reading about that in the Good Parenting guide; and so it has to be a classic case of 'homework on the bus'.

Back in the proper cup, the F.A. type of course the draw has been kind and sends little Emley our way. They are a non league outfit and are about twenty (?) divisions below us (well you try and find them). This is one I have to take the kids to, oh and Phil as he had been behaving himself. I can't resist the chance to have a bet on the outcome, so I go to Corals and fill in my slip with 6-0 and 7-0 selections. The girl behind the counter takes my bet, looks at it and smiles. It's as if she knows that's the last I will see of that. Before I leave the shop one of the punters comes up to me and says "can I give you the winner of the Grand National?" I reply "no you're alright mate; I've only got a little garden". Tickets safely in pocket we set off to witness a goal fest. It doesn't take long for Lampard to fire us in front, here we go now. In fact the goal is so early John Moncur hasn't had time to get booked! But we stutter and underperform and Emley equalise, immediately saving me a return trip to Corals, how very kind of them. The flood gates never opened, in fact the flood was barely a drizzle. Thanks to a late goal from John Hartson our blushes were spared. Grateful for small mercies at least it wasn't a Mansfield, or a Hereford or a Newport. I shall have to stop there as I am getting the flashbacks (nurse the screens).

Towards the end of the season there would be an unusual sequence of games where we played eight and drew seven. Alright so another season has drifted away and we didn't need to buy any silver polish, but two good cup runs and an eighth place finish puts a smile on the face and gives us fresh hope.

My usual Saturday lunch time ritual involves me listening to Dominik Diamond presenting Sports call on radio 5 live. This particular edition there was a competition in which you had to describe your World Cup memory. I took part and my submitted recollection was deemed worthy of first prize. Below is my entry word for word.

My World Cup memory goes back to Mexico in 1970. We had just lost narrowly to Brazil one – nil, but many people believed that they had just witnessed a rehearsal for the final. However in the quarter final we're comfortably two-nil up against West Germany. Then three times the Germans throw their towels over our real life sun lounger Peter Bonetti and we're out. Goalkeeper Gordon Banks did not play that day because he was sick. It must have been contagious as almost immediately the whole country was suffering the same condition, we have just surrendered a two goal lead to the Germans, and oh where is Stan Boardman when you need him.

For that, my efforts were rewarded with a trip to the B.B.C. I had a guided tour of the building which culminated with a visit to the recording studios to meet up with the producer. We had an informal chat about football which he recorded. This was in 1998 just before the World Cup was to begin in France. My thoughts and observations were edited to make a trailer to advertise the matches that were coming up on radio 5 live. So during the day prior to commentaries I could hear myself on the radio promoting the show. The B.B.C. very kindly gave me a copy of the finished recording, move over John Motson. That win has to be one of the one's that gave me the most satisfaction, along with the West Ham shirt. In this competition three of us were on the phone as a commentary of a West Ham game was played. As soon as you recognised the player who was about to score you would then have to shout out your name. It was the first person to correctly identify three goal scorers won a shirt signed by the West Ham team. Those whose signatures were on the shirt were Joe Cole, Shaka Hislop, Paolo Di Canio, Michael Carrick, Steve Lomas, Rio Ferdinand, Frank Lampard, Trevor Sinclair to name but a few. Goalkeeper Bernard Lama never did sign it, but he managed to get a hand to it as it went past him. Yes that was definitely one of the most satisfying competition wins. I've always enjoyed entering competitions and the old adage is perfectly correct 'how can you win the raffle if you don't buy a ticket'?

For financial reasons the following season West Ham would only have the pleasure of my company for three first team fixtures. It is just the kids and I these days as Phil and Debbie have moved to Surrey to run a post office. The first of our two visits was a league cup encounter with Northampton Town. Having been beaten 2-0 in the away leg we have got to go for it. After ninety minutes play all we had to show for our efforts was a solitary Frank Lampard goal to cap a depressing evening. The goal came so late in the proceedings that it was never going to inspire a 'Lazarus' type comeback. The main highlight was being able to see Julian Dicks return after a lengthy lay off. Many people held the opinion that he would never come back after suffering such a serious injury but he proved those doubters wrong. A magnificent personal achievement however could not disguise the fact that he was never going to be the same player. Julian made around a dozen more appearances before his career wearing the claret and blue reached the end of the line.

When an alcoholic goes to an alcoholics anonymous meeting he stands up and says his name followed by, and I am an alcoholic. Well I am standing up, my name is Dave and I like Frank Lampard Junior. As a youngster he had been making a name for himself in the youth and reserve teams with some outstanding performances. He had now stepped up to mix it with the big boys. I realise that I run the risk of alienating myself from a section fans but I am just being honest. Because his dad and uncle held such senior positions of authority at the club he was under an enormous amount of pressure. He had to show he was twice as good as any other player to prove he was worth a place in the starting line up. I felt he coped with that pressure extremely well and performed admirably, and I was not pleased when he was sold. We could and should have benefitted from the player that Chelsea got. Even so I still found amusing the song that the fans would chant at him. It was sung to the tune of One Man Went to Mow and was forever thus:

*Five men couldn't lift*
*Couldn't lift Frank Lampard*
*Five men, four men, three men, two men*
*One man and his forklift truck*
*Couldn't lift Frank Lampard*

A phone in on Capital Gold presents the chance to win seats for the home game with Sheffield Wednesday, and to the victor the spoils. I sell, (sorry give) a ticket to Martin as our visits are not too frequent and I must ensure he keeps the faith. I will have my work cut out convincing him to book a return trip after watching this showing. Benito Carbone tore us apart and we were lucky it ended up just a 4-0 defeat. These two tickets were supposed to have been a winning prize; I do believe the runner-up got four tickets!

We had an almost identical seat in the West Stand upper tier to see Derby County try to wrestle three points away from us. They don't so much wrestle as it's more of a submission as vintage hammers rattle in five goals conceding just the one in the process. Five different goal scorers on a day when the kids ought to be thinking that maybe dad does know what he's on about bringing us here.

Melissa asks me if one of her friends can come to a game with us and I readily agree. I wish that I had paid the fine instead of doing this community service. A not too daunting prospect awaits us in the league cup draw, in the shape of a home game against Bournemouth. Gemma is the friend who makes up the foursome along with me, Melissa and Martin. This would be an ideal choice of game to gently introduce Gemma to the 'inner sanctum', as we are not expecting a full house and tickets are easy to come by. On a cold evening 22,000 of us hardy souls turn up to pay our tributes to strikes from Frank Lampard and Marc Keller in a 2-0 victory. Regardless of seeing us win doesn't stop Gemma from 'slipping through the net' as this was her only visit with us, (are my powers of persuasion deserting me?). A good cup run has always been our best route into Europe, well either that or write a song.

This particular cup run would take us all the way to the semi finals (or would it?). To lose in the semi final is a body blow in itself, but to not even have the chance to contest it because of our own administrative ineptitude beggar's belief. This was a cock up on the scale of a Sunday morning team. In the quarter final we beat Aston Villa on penalties, due in no small way to Gareth Southgate deciding that money was tight and that he needed another pizza commercial, and so chose to miss his penalty. Our elation was short lived lasting no more than twenty four hours, as the next day it became apparent that we had played a 'ringer'. Manny Omoyinmi came on late in the game but he had already played for another club earlier on in this competition. He did not take one of the penalties or contribute much in the few minutes that he had played, but rules are rules. The match was ordered to be replayed and we revert to type and suffer a 3-1 reversal at home. Manny was an adult and surely should have spoken up when selected that he was ineligible. Those in positions of authority at the club should also have been aware as there must have been documentation from the club he was on loan to asking for permission to play him in an earlier round. Office staff and Manny himself lost their jobs as the outcome of this sorry tale. Shutting the door after the horse has bolted brings little consolation, it's too late the damage has been done and we are no longer in the semi final. So a day out at Wembley will be on hold for another day (please god).

On the whole, games against Manchester United are normally worth watching and this one in 1999 would prove the theory to be correct. As usual I was accompanied by that well known double act Melissa and Martin to see if we could stand up to the challenge of the champions elect. At 3-0 down maybe this was a bridge too far, Paolo di Canio disagrees and his two goals give us the kiss of life. He then comes within a whisker of making it 3-3 and then they break away and now it's 4-2. At least we got some self respect back and made a game of it. The Manchester United fans show their ignorance by chanting 'you've only come to see united'. If they had bothered to look at our attendance figures they would have seen that we perform in front of a full house pretty much every home game. Whilst on the subject of Manchester United, it has been widely reported in the press that the Stretford End in their Old Trafford stadium has been threatened with closure.

This is because some fans in that section of the ground refuse to sit down during the matches. I can fully sympathise with their plight and understand why they are doing this; after all it is such a long drive up from Bournemouth that they need to stretch their legs.

I take more than a passing interest in the football phone in shows. Listening to Danny Baker on the Radio 5 live show 6-0-6 I can recall him being in conversation with a man about clubs in financial difficulties, and what sort of state the game was in generally. This dialogue led on to the subject of clubs potentially going out of business.

During their discussion Danny posed the question to the caller, "what would you do if your club went to the wall?" I could not believe my ears on hearing his reply which was "I'd support someone else". I am sitting there thinking whaaaat!-how can you say such a thing? I like to believe that West Ham United will always be around, but if the unthinkable did occur I could not just go and 'nail my colours to the mast' of some other outfit. After respecting their history, the passion and energy, the joy and suffering from following your team I could not comprehend how someone could even think of supporting another team, and then to say so in such a 'matter of fact' way. If there was no West Ham I would still watch games but without the interest. You understand the situation, when you don't want a certain team to win because three points takes them above your favourites, well that would disappear. I would continue to look at the league tables to keep abreast of what was happening. But by and large results and performances would have no great effect on my way of life as I would be a fan of no team. How could you disregard all the games you have seen, memorabilia that you have collected in order to start all over again under someone else's banner. I have spoken to friends who have said they have a 'second team', in essence another side who they quite like and look for their results. Personally I don't have anything of the sort, unless if pushed for an answer my 'second team' would be West Ham reserves.

As I mentioned earlier times are hard as I am between jobs and with Christmas approaching I don't have the funds to buy what I want to get Marie. I make the ultimate sacrifice and 'fall on my sword', yes I sold my autographed West Ham shirt, painful I know but it had to be done.

Maybe I might have been able to get together some cash to pay for myself to get to West Ham but not being able to take the kids along with me the day would have turned into a guilt trip. My reasoning was therefore to put my attendance record on hold for the time being.

# How Did That Happen

The Irons are getting their fair share of T.V. coverage on Sky and next door neighbour Roy keeps the invites coming, all I have to do is to provide the beers. When I return home after watching a game with Roy, Marie says she can always gauge how well we have done as she can hear our cheers echoing through the walls. At home the West Ham wallpaper is coming down in Martin's bedroom, but fear not dear reader the claret and blue paint is ready to go on. This reminds me of the time when Martin was very young and he came home from school one day and asked me how to spell paint, and I replied "what colour?" Back on the decorating front, the top half of the walls I will be painting blue and the lower half claret. This will be offset with the West Ham border paper running round the middle to disguise where the two colours meet. Straight away the value of my property has increased and no, Martin doesn't wake up screaming in the night.

We are watching more reserve games than first team fixtures as the admission price for all three of us comes to only £5. For these matches we have to sit in the East Stand lower as this is the only part of the stadium open to us. Melissa is growing older but still wants to go to West Ham with me which makes me feel good as she is now old enough to make her own choices. However one thing I do find out is that she thinks that I'm nosey; she didn't actually come right out and say that, I read it in her diary.

With my financial situation improving all three of us go to the league cup tie at home to Blackburn Rovers. You may have noticed by now that I always refer to this competition as the league cup. Over the years many different sponsors meant various titles for this tournament, but I'm old school and it will forever remain the league cup to me. Once again we are back at Upton Park in the family enclosure on a freezing cold night. We progress thanks to a 2-0 win but make hard work of what should have been a routine victory; this is one of our more unattractive traits. In the grand scheme of things a win is a win and I'll take that if it keeps us on route to Wembley. A great Christmas pressy was the 5-0 win over Charlton, a quality performance with outstanding goals. Trevor Sinclair's volley being the pick of the bunch. For the final home game of the season I make sure I have the money to take my two young 'disciples' for one last treat as Southampton are coming to town. An eye catching 3-0 win is a fine way to 'sign off'. On this day the presentation is made for the hammer of the year. I was so pleased to see Sebastian Schemmel take the award as I had voted for him. It was a shame that he only stayed for another one and a half seasons. Newspaper reports led us to believe he had a bust-up with manager Glenn Roeder and his race was run. We had lost all three of our previous games so to be there on a day when a 3-0 win is recorded was gratifying in itself.

I was surprised when Roeder got the manager's job as it was reported that he had previously been interviewed for the position and the board felt that he wasn't the right man for the job. Then some weeks later suddenly he's the man that we have been looking for. Go figure.

We didn't exactly hit the ground running in season 2001-02. Five games played and all we have to show for it is one penalty and even a cocktail stick has more points than us. We are going to have a goal of the month competition, if we can get one. I part with a pound to buy a Golden Goal ticket. If you are not familiar with this concept then please allow me to explain. When you open the ticket inside is printed a time in minutes and seconds, for example you may see 16.11. If the first goal of the game goes in at that particular time it's then happy days and drink up you have won. So having purchased my golden goal ticket I open it up to see it doesn't have a time in it, it just says NOVEMBER.

Unbelievably we let in twelve goals in two games and Shaka Hislop in goal is getting a bad back with all that bending down picking the ball out of the net. Thankfully the tide turns and three wins on the bounce puts us back on track. A feast of goals for Sky television to savour as we draw 4-4 away at Charlton. I'm watching next door with Roy and when I return home Marie says she had no chance of an early night with all the shouting and screaming coming through the walls.

Middlesbrough come to Upton Park and so do me and Martin thanks again to local radio. Reading the team line up's, I'm pleased to see that Hayden Foxe has been omitted from our starting eleven, as I have never rated the man. To my mind the better option was Hannu Thihen. Each of us have our favourites, and there are others who we are not so keen on. You have yours and I have mine and it's all a matter of opinion. But I have always held the belief that beauty is in the eye of the beer-holder. There were three players who we chased hard to sign, Hayden Foxe, Ilie Dumitrescu and Vladimir Labant. Plenty of problems were met when trying to secure work permits but assurances were given to the fans stating all the hassle would be worth it to sign these 'top players'. I'm afraid to say all the aforementioned were a total let down to me. This is Alex Bunbury all over again and I'm not impressed. Meanwhile if you're still waiting for the result from the Middlesbrough game it's just come in, a single strike from Freddie Kanoute has earned us three points. This will start a run of the final twelve games in which we will score in eleven of them and that's more like it. Dawn and false are two words that spring to mind.

Season 2002-03 begins and after nine games we haven't even got enough points to stop us from driving. At Christmas we are bottom of the league, but looking at our squad you would think we have enough quality players to avoid the drop. It's a dangerous game this thinking. Come February and we are in nineteenth position and I am still wearing my brown trousers. The final eleven games will see us beaten only once, but the damage has been done in the first half of the season. Most seasons fourty two points is good enough to keep you in the 'promised land', but not on this occasion as we swap Match of the Day for the football league show.

# Good Friends are Like the Stars

Even though we have been relegated Trevor Brooking's three games in charge produced wins over Manchester City and Chelsea and a draw away at Birmingham. While managing on a temporary basis he had certainly shown some promise, so much so that when the new season kicks off he is still in the hot seat. Many questions have to be answered, does he want the job on a permanent basis, can he take us back up, will there be a 'fire sale' of our best talent as in previous years, and exit signs are they on the way out, (sorry I just got carried away there for a moment). In the past we had sold off 'the family silver' in the shape of Joe Cole, Michael Carrick, Jermain Defoe, Glen Johnson, Rio Ferdinand, Frank Lampard and Sinclair and Kanoute won't be getting a testimonial here either. Trevor Brooking kept the seat warm for another twelve games of which only one would end in defeat. He was adamant that he didn't want the post full time as he did not want to sour the wonderful relationship he had built up with the fans.

I can understand his thinking on this one as the day would arrive (as it always does) when it's all going wrong and fans would be calling for his head. That is the nature of the beast that nothing good lasts forever. He has steadied the ship and can walk away with his head held high and legendary status intact. The inevitability of a manager's demise is the only reason I'd like to see Julian Dicks at the helm. Because when the fateful day arrives and the fans can take no more it would be quite surreal to hear thousands of guy's chanting Dicks out!

Another competition win comes my way this time by way of a local newspaper, and my reward is two seats at the London Master's six a side tournament. Martin will be my travelling companion and we head off to the Docklands Arena. This tournament is different from the one that I organised trips to many moons ago. For a start this will not be a straight forward knock out competition as the teams are divided into groups. This innovation guarantees us seeing the hammers play a minimum of at least three games which I am all in favour of. Another difference is that the ball can go above head height, whereas in the five a side version the restriction was knee height. We field a strong side with players having to be thirty-five years plus to take part. Ours include Tony Cottee, Frank Mcavennie, Ian Bishop, Martin Allen, Ray Stewart and Alvin Martin. What I didn't like was the introduction of the 'Americanism' style music. When a team were on the attack over the tannoy system they would play cavalry charge style music. This event took place on a Sunday afternoon and we both had a great time. This was mainly because the lads seemed fired up and keen to do well. We comfortably won our group and were scoring freely. This enabled us to qualify for the final to do battle with Charlton. Extra time had failed to produce a winner and the scores were locked at 1-1, and now for the dreaded penalty shoot-out. When Ray Stewart stepped up I explained to Martin that this was a given, quickly describing his temperament, accuracy and impressive scoring record. This is the man to put your mortgage on. I had just enough time to finish extolling his virtues before watching him miss and we are runner's up. What is it they say 'the curse of the commentator'. As it was a Sunday the journey home was rubbish with buses in for trains.

Back in the world of the eleven a side game we have to come to terms with the fact that we are down, and recognise that our new manager Alan Pardew will want to stamp his mark on the club and create his own team. Taking that into consideration I still never expected a total of thirty six players to feature in our line up this season. It was obvious that some would want to get away as soon as possible, a move that I do not agree with. They were responsible for getting us relegated, and then to walk away with the attitude of 'you can get on with it' doesn't sit well with me. I would suggest in the event of relegation it should be written in their contract that they have to stay for at least one season to try and repair the damage they have caused.

Bradford City was the first match I went to taking Martin along with me. Naturally the hammers fans stay loyal (never doubted them for a moment) and the crowd is in excess of 30,000. A Defoe strike from twenty yards gives us the chance to celebrate another three points in the bag. The abiding memory from this fixture was when we arrived at Barking station on the journey home. A fan who had drunk enough for all of us was 'singing' at the top of his voice to the tune of blue moon 'there's only one Defoe' for almost ten minutes, we were so happy to see the train arrive. Defoe had earlier put in a transfer request but was still with us. He hadn't actually come out and stated that he was refusing to play, but by getting himself sent off three times before Christmas meant he wasn't spending too much time on the pitch anyway. Once again Essex radio comes to my rescue as I win two seats for our home game where we take on Burnley. In order to win these the listeners are required to listen out to when a pre – determined song was played and that would be the cue to call. The listener who happened to be on lucky line thirteen would claim the spoils. My lucky streak shows no sign of deserting me as I make more work for the postman. Right now I sense that I could fall into a barrel of manure and still come up smelling of roses.

It had been far too many years since I had met up with any of the lads from the days of the famous five. So with that in mind I gave a call to Dave Craft to enquire if he wanted the spare ticket for the Burnley affair, and much to my delight he said yes. Before the game he arrived at our house for a spot of lunch and it was good to reminisce of times gone by before catching the train from Basildon. He was still in contact with Trevor, and he likewise with Steve. Ian had quit the insurance business and had taken a long distance lorry driving job, with all the Yorkies you can eat. Furthermore, he had also purchased a property abroad and was spending more time out of the country (I always wanted to be a tax exile too). We had not met up for some while but the friendship was still there. Having made that initial contact again we are all still friends to this day I'm happy to say. Friends are like the stars; you don't always see them but they are always there. That is what makes true friends despite the time lapse all of us still wanted to be mates. Dave and I had so much to catch up on with reference to work, family and home life in general the day passed by so quickly. As for the Burnley game it finished honours even as both sides shared four goals. A late strike from Don Hutchison was our get out of jail card. Dave and I continued our conversation about the old days over a beer when we returned to mine. Marie chose to take a sip of mine and remarked "that's awful; I don't know how you can drink that stuff". To which I replied "my point exactly- when I'm out you think I'm enjoying myself".

Life is too short to lose touch with friends and with that thought in mind it encourages me to give Phil Parmenter a call. Pleasantries are exchanged and the conversation turns to the important issues of the world, West Ham's recent fortunes. During this discussion Phil informs me his family will be making the pilgrimage to Upton Park when we host Wigan Athletic and am I interested in going. A delay of a second and a half was followed by my reply of "yes, and can you get me three seats?" Phil and Debbie have two children like we do and we agree that this extracurricular activity is vital in their upbringing and education to make them better people. He gets the requested three tickets for me Melissa and Martin. In the upper tier of the East Stand we have a great view as we watch the irons maul Wigan 4-0. Prior to the kick off I somehow found myself in Corals and noticed the odds on a 4-0 home win were 20/1 and decided to risk a pound. On my return to Corals I had to ask a punter where the paying out window was as it had been so long since I had a win I had forgotten the way. Marlon Harewood had already scored twice when with not long to go he was clean through, one on one with the keeper. Now I experience a rare moment going on in my head as I'm thinking to myself please don't let him score. At 4-0 the game was in the bag and I didn't want him to ruin my outing to Corals (cheers Marlon).

With the transfer of so many players in and out the side is not a settled one which hampers our quest for automatic promotion. Most of the signings are 'journeyman players rather than stand out star acquisitions. Our transfer dealings give me the impression that we are now shopping in Aldi's rather than Waitrose. Irrespective of this we still are able to get to the play offs. Paired with Ipswich

Town we travel to Portman Road for the first leg and suffer a one goal defeat. In the grand scheme of things that's not too shabby. The second leg at Upton Park was a magical night and it most definitely took me back to those nights when we were playing in the European Cup Winners Cup. Melissa and I were there to sample this special atmosphere that would inspire the lads to a 2-0 victory. Mattie Etherington smashed home a 'worldie' and Christian Daily plundered the killer goal to put us in the play-off final in Cardiff where we will play Crystal Palace. I never went to the game but watching it on television was painful viewing. We just never got going and the overall performance was well below our usual standard. The manager's substitutions seemed somewhat strange to me. In a must win game where we are trailing 1-0 and are desperate for a goal, he takes off our strikers. Needless to say that plan went up in smoke and Crystal Palace emerge with a 1-0 win and promotion is theirs. What a cup competition that was, we had to play fourty six games just to get to the semi-final.

# **Playing Escalator Football**

At this point in her life Melissa has a steady boyfriend and he is a gooner. Always prepared to do our bit for Care in the Community we take him with us to watch the mid-week cup tie against Southend United. Hopefully showing him the finer things in life will help improve his education and we can release him back into civilisation. He has been used to singing 'one nil to the Arsenal', but tonight he has to sing 'two nil to the cockney boys'. Two goals from Marlon Harewood and its job done and for me Melissa and Martin a laughter filled journey home.

We are extremely grateful for the home draws we get in recent years as it makes the job of getting tickets a whole lot easier compared to league matches. Friday night is an unusual time for us to schedule a home league encounter but two weeks before Christmas there is one on the fixture list and Leeds United are coming out to play. This proves a popular attraction with the fans as close on 31,000 fans are in attendance, which proves the point, give the people what they want (West Ham United) and they will come. Luke Chadwick's goal was not enough to clinch all three points as a last gasp penalty salvaged a point for our northern 'friends'. I went to this game with Martin and having just witnessed our three points converted back into one we left our seats rather dejectedly. On a positive note we remain a top six side. Apart from the first couple of weeks we have been there or thereabouts all season. Teddy Sheringham's experience is a huge plus and his consistent good form will rightly earn him the player of the year title. Nigel Reo Coker's enthusiasm and mid field drive was another contributory factor towards our quest for promotion. I do feel he should have gone on to be a better player than he was. Later in life he wrote that he made a huge mistake leaving us when he did (if only he had asked me). Martin and I make our way home after the Leeds match and we wait at Barking station for our train. It's a cold night so it's a welcome relief to see the train pull in after just a few minutes wait. Eagerly we get aboard, race to get a seat and begin to discuss our sadness at letting three points slip away. We look up to notice that sitting directly opposite us are Martin's school headmaster and his son who are both Leeds United fans smiling broadly in the knowledge they have just stolen a point from us. What were the chances of that; of all the people who could have sat there we get two Leeds fans. Once again automatic promotion has eluded us but at least we have the next best thing, the consolation prize of the play offs.

Yet again we are paired with Ipswich Town. For this most important of games Melissa would be my travelling companion. Racing into a 2-0 advantage leads us to assume this will be a formality and makes the palms less sweaty. Even after all these years I still can't get used to the fact that we like to do things the hard way. We allow Ipswich to claw their way back into the tie with two goals and keep the pot boiling for the second leg. Isn't it nice of us to keep the interest there for all concerned, rather than put the tie to bed in the first leg (I don't think). But as Baden Powell always said when describing West Ham –be prepared. Our performance at Portman Road is a joy to behold; a wonderful 2-0 win and its back to Wales (please drive Caerphilly).

Yet again we have used over thirty players to get us to the final; such are the demands of a long season in this division. A surging run and cross from Mattie Etherington presents Bobby Zamora with the chance to become a hero which he thankfully took. This added to his three goals in the semi-final made it a fantastic end to the campaign for Zamora. I never went to the final but after the big let down the previous year I was thrilled for the fans that did. With all the riches that playing with the 'big boys' bring a second successive near miss would have been unbearable. Many of the games I have chosen to comment on are selected from the ones that I actually went to. This year would see me set an unwanted record as for the first time since 'I don't know when' I manage not one single visit. Next door neighbour Roy is still providing a safe haven for my TV. Fix, and as we are featured quite a lot I'm still there with you in spirit guys. The reasons for my absence are twofold. Firstly, it is now becoming more difficult to get tickets, and secondly we are to move house once more which I am sure you can appreciate is a costly venture. I try to convince Roy to buy the house next door to us when we move but alas my plans are thwarted. At this juncture it seems an opportune moment to recall an incident when new neighbours moved in next door to us. He called round to introduce himself and asked me the question when I decorated my lounge how many rolls of wallpaper did I get, to which I replied "nine". Two weeks later he called again and said "when I asked you how many rolls of wallpaper you got for your lounge you said nine". "That's right" I responded. "Well I've got two left over" he said. "So have I", was my unwelcome reply.

Anyway back to matters in hand we are playing up in the top tier again after more ups and down's than an escalator and there's more to come. We are most definitely 'eye candy' on the pitch. The player who impresses me the most is Yossi Benayoun, he reminds me a lot of Eyal Berkovic. Players who have that extra something to unlock a tight defence, to go past another player, or to find that killer pass to create a goal scoring opportunity will always get my vote. Dean Ashton is looking the real deal up front and England will come calling. Melissa is now going to games without me so I consider my work is done, a triumph for my parenting skills. The obvious highlight of this season is the fantastic cup run that takes us all the way to the final where Liverpool lie in wait. For the third year in a row we are going to Wales. There ought to be a sign erected on the A13 reading WEST HAM TWIN TOWN WITH CARDIFF. Unable to get any tickets for the final I'm not too unhappy because in my heart of hearts I feel that I don't really deserve one due to my poor attendance record. The travelling fans should always take priority, those who went to Bolton, Manchester City and the semi final at Villa Park. On a more positive note despite the fact that Melissa does not live with us any more she decides to come round and we watch the final as a family, a lovely gesture that was greatly appreciated. The game was a classic, 3-3 after extra time only for us to experience the heartache of losing the penalty shoot out. We were just a matter of seconds away from winning the trophy in normal time. The clock is ticking down and time added on has almost expired and then Steven Gerrard scores the type of goal that only comes along once in a lifetime, WHY DID IT HAVE TO BE IN MINE. In extra time we had come so close to snatching a winner, even hitting the post but when it's not meant to be your day what can you do? If you are going to get beat then there are ways to lose. I was devastated because we had been beaten, but at the same time proud of the boys in the manner of the defeat. They gave everything, playing with pride and passion and came so close. On the morning of the game I was in Corals to check what odds they were offering on us and a hammers win was marked up at 4/1. Straight away I am thinking I need to get some of the kids money on this (no of course I wasn't really thinking that). What I was thinking was, that's tempting I'm having a slice of that. So it was my hard earned cash that found its way over the counter never to be seen again. I, like West Ham had come so close. At the time when Gerrard's 'missile' flew past Shaka Hislop into our net I realised my luck was so bad that if I had been one of Kelly Brook's triplets I would have been the one on the bottle.

Some consolation was that even in defeat we have still qualified for European football next season as Liverpool are also there. I find coping with defeat is easier to manage nowadays. When I was younger a West Ham defeat would ruin my whole weekend, and in the words of Danny Dyer 'I would 'ave the right 'ump 'and my mood was certainly not good (remember Anderlecht). Going to work on a Monday morning was a whole lot easier after a win on the Saturday. When the children were younger and I was taking them I was forever worried that if they saw us losing on a regular basis that their interest would drain away. To illustrate my point that Sheffield Wednesday 4-0 game is a perfect example. I had seen this situation before and my loyalty was never going to waiver. But with youngsters it's different. Classmates who follow whoever is at the top of the table are quick to offer the advice to come and support a winning team. It's about so much more than that but you do not realise this until you are older. The younger generation are impressionable but thankfully my two have stayed faithful to the claret and blue persuasion. There was one interesting statistic that emerged from this season.

An all too frequent joke at our expense was that West Ham came down with the Christmas decorations. We dispel that theory as from the beginning of January we record seven wins on the bounce.

# We're All in a Spin

The following season both West Ham and I are all over the place. Let us take the hammers plight first. The joy of being back in Europe is short lived as before the end of September we have fallen at the first hurdle, failing to get past the Italian side Palermo who with a 4-0 aggregate under their belt were worthy winners. In my formative years I used to speak Italian, when I arrived home from school I would shout out "mum I'm 'ere." That comprehensive defeat would leave us free to concentrate on the league is the statement I trot out in these situations to console myself as I assume that it is what you are supposed to do. West Ham had lured us in to a false sense of security after the first four games. Bobby Zamora had netted in every game and we had only tasted defeat once. Now was a good time to go out and order some more wheels as they were about to come off.

After those encouraging opening four games we then go on to endure eight straight defeats, scoring a measly one goal in the process. To make matters worse it would be twenty three more games before Bobby Zamora gets congratulated for hitting the back of the net. If I remember correctly it featured on a television programme-Tales of the

Unexpected. Somebody buy him a compass. All of these factors contributed to the downfall of Alan Pardew and he was subsequently relieved of his duties. He was to be replaced by ex-hammer Alan Curbishley who had worked wonders by keeping Charlton in the top flight for so long. We were destined to spend all of the season hovering over the relegation trap door. Two class players had signed on the dotted line and now we had secured the ownership of Tevez and Mascherano, or had we? This debate would rumble on and eventually cost us thousands of pounds and very nearly our premiership status. Was it West Ham or a third party company who owned the players contracts which was the burning issue. To my amazement, amongst all this controversy the two players in question would hardly feature. Were we really that good that we could afford to leave two quality signings on the sidelines? The simple answer to that is no we weren't, so that is that problem dealt with. In actual fact instead of signing these two we should have been trying to sign Tom Cruise as this was going to be Mission Impossible.

The Tevez influence finally kicks in and we go on an amazing run in which we win seven of our final nine matches to stay in the division. West Ham you are ageing me before my time. Sheffield

United are so happy we are staying up that they want to put it in all the papers. We were so grateful for all the publicity they got for us, that we gave them a few million pounds. It becomes apparent that any chance of success will have to come by way of one of the cups.

Speaking of cups, it has for a long while been a dream of mine to be able take my kids to see the hammers play in the cup final. So far the closest we have come to that experience is when I took them to watch us play in the final of the Inter-Toto cup. This would have been in 1999 and the winners were to be rewarded with entry into the Europa league. The French side Metz were our opposition that night as we sat in the Trevor Brooking upper tier for the first leg of the final. The stadium was full of expectant fans and even then we did things the hard way. Once again we shoot ourselves in the foot as Frank Lampard misses a penalty in a 1-0 reverse. The three of us return home with faces longer than the M6. In the away leg it's a completely different story and a 3-1 scoreline enables us to lift the trophy and march into Europe.

I am starting to lose more time from work with health problems. I am having dizzy spells and now they are becoming more frequent and lasting longer. For this reason Upton Park is a no go area for me. My doctor prescribes various types of medication as he thinks that I may have Vertigo. None of these are beneficial to me and so suggests a visit to the hospital. I am subjected to balance and hearing tests and attacks are even induced by pouring water into the inner ear. The outcome was to have a Grommet fitted in the ear alas no joy with that procedure. The next course of action was to have a series of Steroid injections; these were injected directly into my ear and were extremely painful. After six visits to have this treatment there was still no sign of any improvement. Basildon hospital had done all they could for me and referred me to Addenbrookes hospital in Cambridge. Luckily for me Dave Craft being the good friend that he is drove me there. After this initial visit the hospital would then provide a car ambulance for all my future appointments. My attacks had grown to be more severe and more frequent. I was now suffering badly and underwent a period of six months where I had an attack every day; I will try to describe the feeling for you.

It wasn't a gradual slow spinning, it was as though a switch had been flicked in my head and everything would be flying around. When this happened at home I would be clinging on to the chair for dear life as the room was violently spinning. I was constantly being sick and the sensation was that I was upside down and each attack could last anything up to ten hours. In order to try and restrict these attacks I am advised to avoid Caffeine, alcohol, chocolate and excessive fluid intake and salt. The doctor suggested Gentamicin injected into the ear might help, but if this did not work that I would lose all sense of hearing in that ear. I could no longer put up with the attacks and chose to go for this option. In my case it did not work and now I am deaf in one ear. Walking has become an issue; it feels as though I am walking on a trampoline. Inside my head it's a constant battle to remain upright causing severe headaches. When the attacks first began I had the presence of mind to grab hold of something to stop myself from falling now I find myself unable to do this, and I am hitting the floor before I know it. At work I have one really nasty fall where I sprained my wrist, cracked a rib and cut my head, and the paramedics had to be called to sort me out. In between attacks I am trying to go about my business living my life only to suffer the indignation of collapsing in two shops, those being H.M.V. and Boots and on both occasions the staff were very kind and helpful. This was extremely embarrassing as people not knowing of my condition more than likely assumed that I was either drunk or on drugs as I was all over the place. One time when an attack happened I was in the street clinging on to a lamppost for dear life as everything was upside down and spinning. A total stranger came up to see if I was o.k. I tried my best to explain that I wasn't and he got me to his car and drove me home and restoring my faith in human nature. There really are some good people out there after all. On my next visit to the Vertigo clinic at Addenbrookes I discuss these symptoms with the doctor and he makes it known to me that what I am experiencing are called 'Drop Attacks', that were causing me to hit the deck before I knew what was happening. Another procedure called Dixhall Pyke was tried on me, this involved the doctor getting my head in a certain position whilst I am lying on the bed and then quickly twisting it in order to release trapped crystals. For a brief period it was an improvement then the symptoms would re-appear. My condition was now known as menieres disease and an operation seemed to be the only option left, and I was booked in for a Saccus Decompression. I had to attend a pre- op assessment where the procedure was explained to me and I was given the opportunity to ask questions. A hole was going to be drilled and a plastic tube would be inserted to facilitate drainage and remains in the mastoid. This operation should be about two hours. The surgeon asked me if I was nervous and quite naturally I said yes. He then asked why that was to which I responded, "on the way in I noticed that out the front you have a large sign saying Guard Dogs Operating Here. Now I know you have cut backs but that doesn't inspire me". That made him smile and he continued to talk me through what was going to happen. During this line of questioning he went on to enquire if I had undergone any previous operations and did they go o.k. So I informed him I had previously had a vasectomy and that it did not go alright. With a puzzled look on his face he wanted to know what happened, so I told him that I only went in to have my tonsils out and some bugger turned the trolley round! A bit of gallows humour to lighten the mood and now we are getting on fine. He had answered all of my questions; put me at my ease and now I am counting down the days until my operation. Come the day of my operation and I'm lying on the bed in my gown, waiting to be put to sleep ready to go into theatre. It was at this moment that I chose to have a quick word with those around me and told them "I know why you lot are all wearing masks, "to which one of them said "why". My reply was "because if it goes wrong I don't know who done it". And with that it was good night from me as they put the mask over my face, and I was off to sleep dreaming of West Ham winning the Champions League (this is sure strong stuff, what is it they have given me). Thankfully all went well and I would have a better quality of life for a while after a few years of suffering, but that would not be the end of that particular story. A couple of week's recovering, some medication for a month and I was back at work, and yes when I did return to work I did have to sign the visitor's book.

# A Change is Good as a Mess

In the Eastgate shopping centre in Basildon a new shop has opened up dealing in sports memorabilia. Looking in the window I am instantly drawn to a large framed picture of Bobby Moore, Julian Dicks, Paolo di Canio, Billy Bonds and Trevor Brooking (well who wouldn't be). Deciding this will look great on my living room wall I venture inside. The assistant comes over to serve me and it's none other than Steve Jones our former striker. It's not too busy in the shop and he has time to chat, and yes we did talk about that sensational strike at White Hart Lane in a 4-1 win. He was very honest when relating how his career had turned out, and that he was still in contact with some of his old team mates as he played for West Ham in the six a side masters. Having explained to me that his time at Upton Park was all too short I was quick to remind him that it is better to be a has been than a never was.

Even though Carlos Tevez had left we had Dean Ashton and Craig Bellamy up front I reckoned we would have no problems in that department. Over the course of the season we average just over one goal per game and shoot's my theory down in flames. In Bellamy's case we saw him about as often as Halleys comet. It wasn't the greatest squad we had ever assembled and when players were being released behind his back manager Curbishley obviously thought that he was being undermined and quit. Round about this time I noticed that the West Ham nights were attracting more publicity and proving immensely popular. As a birthday surprise Marie had booked tickets for me to go to one at the Brentwood Leisure Centre. I went with Melissa's 'latest squeeze' at the time who was also a hammers fan (now she's getting the hang of how to pick a boyfriend).

These events mainly took place in theatres and would involve ex-hammers appearing on stage and talking about their life and times in claret and blue. The players under the spotlight when we went were Tony Cottee and Billy Bonds. A full house was given an interesting insight into behind the scenes affairs. As the host, Tony Gale prompted the pair with questions that would lead to anecdotes he knew we would love to hear. The two Tony's appeared more comfortable and natural in the role of speaker, and were trying their utmost to bring 'Bonzo' out of his shell. A very entertaining evening and given the opportunity I will happily go to another such function.

The lads continue to meet up to keep in touch with how we are all doing but it never takes long for the conversation to be steered back to West Ham events past and present. This gives Dave a chance to re-live one of his favourite tales. This one particular time we are travelling on the tube for a home game. The carriage is packed solid and we are all standing. For this game a guy called Keith was with us, and I believe he was more of a mate of Dave and Trevor's. As I was saying we were all squashed together like sardines and a moments silence fell on the proceedings. In that split second Dave turned to Keith and said "if you don't stop touching my arse I'm going to give you such a slap". Almost immediately you could hear a sharp intake of breath from the other passengers. They were looking at Keith, pointing and muttering under their breath. Keith was so embarrassed he went bright red and to cap it all he only went and got off at the next stop. We met up with him later but he had fallen victim to yet another Dave Craft wind-up.

A story that Trevor is proud to relate revolved around a trip to Stamford Bridge to see us play Chelsea. This goes back to the late 1970's (and so does the last time Trevor got a round in), I wasn't at this game as at the time I was back playing on

Saturdays. Trevor and Dave were in the shed end. This was during the era when Doc Martens were the footwear of choice for many a fan. The police wanted to reduce the risk of trouble and so upon entering the stadium, fans were told to remove the laces from their boots. Being West Ham fans in the Chelsea end didn't go down too well with Mr. Plod and they were kindly invited to leave. As a local derby often demands there was a heavy police presence many of whom were on horseback. Dave and Trevor lace up their boots and then proceed to take all the laces belonging to the Chelsea supporters. As I am sure you can imagine where there are a lot of horses, there's going to be plenty of horse shit. This was an opportunity too good to miss, and so they trampled all the laces belonging to the Chelsea fans into the horse shit. That must have slowed them down on their journey home.

However, there wasn't too much to smile about on the pitch. Foreign players coming and going many who in my opinion were never going to stay and improve the squad. The likes of Di Michiele, Boa Morte Kovac Lasuuka, Lopez, Savio and Tristan were some I never had time for. The trend would continue for me into the next season and again I'm less than impressed with Fazio, Di Costa, Franco and Mido. Whoever is recommending all these imports to us needs to be re-united with their P45. West Ham are providing my workmates with plenty of ammunition to offload in my direction. My Upton Park attendance record is poor and if it was on a report card it would warrant, must try harder see me later. But you don't have to be inside the ground to feel the pain of a defeat. Manager Gianfranco Zola has tried his best to no avail and is shown the door.

We host Millwall in the league cup and as there is no love lost between the two sets of fans there are regrettably scenes of violence. There is a mass brawl in Green Street with many injuries. The next day while I am at work a delivery driver calls to drop off some parcels. He wastes no time in telling me that all West Ham fans are mindless hooligans. At once I rise to the bait and tell him that it wouldn't bother me if I was arrested by the police, charged and sent to prison as I would be out in next to no time. When he asked me how that would be possible I told him "because my wife never lets me finish a sentence".

Compared to his replacement Avram Grant, then Zola was a genius. Grant was an awful manager seeming unable to do anything right. If he fell out of bed I very much doubt if he could hit the floor. If success breeds success, then we must be on the pill. Now we are going to have to learn to take the rough with the rougher. With Demba Ba starting only ten games and scoring seven goals to be our leading goal scorer tells its own story. I have a friend who is a Manchester United supporter (I'm not proud I'll talk to anyone) and I tell him that the difference between Manchester United and West Ham is that you've got a manager who's one in a million, whereas we have a manager who's won in a raffle. This was going to be a fairy tale season – GRIMM! Mark Noble and Scott Parker gave their best but we were carrying too many passengers. The squad expands to thirty seven, we win just seven league games and our leading goal scorer has narrowly missed out on the golden boot award with his (HAUL) of seven goals.

Halfway through the season we are led to believe that Martin o' Neil is ready to answer our S.O.S. (save our season) but we manage to mess that one up and the inevitable happens. The board have dropped a bollock, we have dropped a division and Marie has dropped a dress size.

Our one and only crumb of comfort in this turbulent season came via the league cup. We are in the semi-final and in typical fashion we once again snatch defeat from the jaws of victory. In the second leg at Birmingham we hold a 3-1 advantage with just the second half remaining. We then concede three and the Wembley dream is put to bed for another year.

When the lads meet up West Ham give us so much to talk about. Another West Ham evening is planned at the Towngate theatre in Basildon and the lads are up for this one and get me a ticket. As sods law often dictates I have another attack of Menieres and I am too ill to go. As they are more advanced than Vertigo this is why my visits to the Boleyn ground have been curtailed. The financial situation in Iceland (the country, not the supermarket) didn't help the club with players on large contracts putting the club in financial turmoil. The owners promised the earth and delivered very little, almost running the club into the ground. Things had to change from the top.

# **Bolton in Disguise**

The medication that I am taking to combat the Menieres Syndrome seems to be having an effect. The attacks still occur, but the degree of severity has lessened. Any positive no matter how small is gratefully accepted by me. These have restricted me back to the role of an armchair fan, but nonetheless still a fan. I go to Dave's and Trevor's to watch us on Sky and return the invite when we are on terrestrial television. Watching with friends is more enjoyable when you can discuss and share opinions, plus the fact the banter with these lads cheers me up no end.

Having moved to Surrey Phil Parmenter was working in Basildon while Debbie ran the post office. We met up and during our conversation he tells me he has joined the local social club and as a member he can sign me in. He then goes on to suggest the next time Sky show the hammers I should go and watch it with him and some of his mates. It was an easy decision to accept as we always got on so well. The game I went along to watch was an away fixture at Manchester City which we lose 3-1. At the final whistle we held our own counselling discussion with fellow suffers and addicts. We form our own self-help group and meet twice a week! The result aside it was good to meet up with an old friend once more. Speaking of old friends (and they don't come much older than him), Mike the Queens Park Rangers fan comes round to see how I'm getting on. We go back years and are more than happy to have a go at each other's teams, always in jest. I know deep down he has a soft spot for the irons, after the rangers result it's always our score he looks for. He regards us as a sort of adopted second team. While he is here I tell him that Queens Park Rangers have a live game coming up on Sky TV, and that since this has been announced more televisions have been sold than ever before. He answered "is that so?" I then said "yes, I've sold mine, my neighbour has sold his, my brother-in-law has sold his" He took it in good spirit and we are due to meet in court next month. Ian is the only one of our crowd that I hardly ever see. I know that he is living out in Boreham and if I can get my visa sorted out I will go and pay him a call (I think he is doing missionary work out there). As far as I know he is still a season ticket holder.

When Windsor Castle burnt down the Queen described it as an Annus Horribulus which translated into 'a terrible year'. Well we have just had an Anus Horribulus 'an arsehole of a year'.

From the end of August we were languishing in twentieth position and stayed in and around there all season and it came as no surprise when we went down. Some days you are the statue, and some days you are the pigeon. But with the ill-fated Bond Scheme, wasting Rio's transfer money 'manny gate', and selling all the promising young players, West Ham can come up with numerous ways to make sure we are the ones turned to stone.

Sam Allardyce is the next cab off the rank and comes with a reputation for keeping teams in the premier division. But if you want to be entertained in the process don't hold your breath. My overall opinion on his appointment is every silver lining has a cloud. In come seven players with a Bolton pedigree, and when I say the word pedigree I use it incorrectly.

Only two victories in the first five outings was only average. Personally I was more upset to see Scott Parker leave. He had been a stand out consistent performer who richly deserved his player of the year awards. He was so unfortunate not to go to the world cup finals with England. Dave, Trevor and I need to inspect big Sam's methods from closer quarters and purchase tickets for the home game where we welcome Peterborough United. Typically on the train journey I have a mild attack and we have to sit on the station for a while until it eases. I am better at organising attacks than Sam is. Dave has a ticket that won't activate the turnstile and allow him to get in and join me inside the stadium. He turns to Trevor and say's "let me try your ticket", Trevor swaps tickets with Dave and this works and Dave is inside with me. The only problem now is Trevor is outside unable to get in having swapped tickets with Dave. We told him we were going in to see the game and would meet up later, instead we found a steward to come and sort his ticket out to get him in.

I'm wondering how best to describe to you my first reaction to an Allardyce performance. It was one of those 'thrill an hour' games. Ten minutes had elapsed when Mark Noble confidently tucks home a spot kick to calm any early nerves. We sit prepared to watch us press on and make the most of our early advantage. This doesn't materialise and we seem to be playing as if there are only ten minutes left and we are desperate to defend our lead. Long balls pumped in the direction of our lone striker Carlton Cole, with little or no support are returned all too quickly. In the second half we notice striker John Carew preparing to come on. We all agree that's better

Sam's going for it now playing two up front. How wrong we were as Cole comes off to leave us playing the same system just different personnel. From a good early start we hold on to win 1-0. First impressions, three points but not easy on the eye, but then again we knew what we were getting.

Sam says he doesn't know what the West Ham way is; I would have respected him more had he acted in a more honest way. By that I mean he could have said something along the lines of, I understand the West Ham way but we may have to put it on hold for a season as I believe that style of play might not get us out of this division right now. Or alternatively admitting that his forte is not organising attacking sides, and that he likes his teams to be based on defensive qualities. Perhaps he thinks our normal style of play would lead to defeats and the crowd would stay away. West Ham fans are loyal and that would not happen.

When relegated under John Lyall and Billy Bonds they returned us to the top division without compromising our footballing principles in front of healthy crowds. I am fully aware that in this division the football is a bit 'harem- scarem' with not too much time allowed on the ball. Maybe if Sam's methods get us up he might re-evaluate the situation next season. I can but hope, after all I want to be entertained and he is in the results business. Hopefully we can find some common ground somewhere in between. Things may well have turned out differently if Tony Cottee's plan had come to fruition. He had been searching far and wide for West Ham fans wealthy enough to invest in the club and be part of a consortium ready to take over. After coming so close he had the rug pulled from underneath him by the Icelandic businessmen, who having shown an initial interest in his proposals then went ahead with their own deal.

A lot of our money was wasted and nearly brought the club to its knees. We have a lot to thank David Gold, David Sullivan and Karren Brady for. Back in the day directors would pump money into their club for no other reason than they loved their club, many never expecting any return. Whereas in this day and age running a football club is big business, you have to be viable and show a profit. I've never seen a balance sheet but I get the impression that we are now on an even keel.

Even though we have dropped a division we are a big fish in a small pond and continue to get our fair share of television coverage. A long hard season ends with us yet again in the play-offs. Trevor had risked a few bob on us to get promotion and so was still in with a chance of forcing William Hill's into liquidation. In the two legged semi-final versus Cardiff we win both the home and away games by an aggregate of 5-0 and this time the final would be played at Wembley. Trevor can now go to B and Q to purchase a wheelbarrow ready to carry his winning's home in. Blackpool will be joining us in the final, and having rattled in eight goals past them in the two league fixtures we are firm favourites. A lifetime of supporting the hammers brings two words to mind, chickens and count. Trevor, Dave and I try our best to get hold of some tickets but as we are no longer regulars at Upton Park this is proving to be no easy task. I was asking everyone I knew, friend's workmates neighbours etc. saying that I was after three tickets. One friend did come good and told me he was able to get me a ticket which I had to refuse. There were three of us trying to go together and I couldn't turn round and say I'm o.k. I've got my ticket; I wanted to go with them so it had to be three or none at all.

On the day of the final Dave's daughter Lisa (who has Sky T.V.) was going out and offered us her front room for the game. So given the choice of going to Wembley on my own or watching it on television with my mates it was no contest. I have lost count of the number of times I have left Upton

Park saying "we played well and didn't deserve to lose that one". Today was to be a role reversal as we should have been wearing black and white hooped shirts as we stole this one. Inside the first half hour Blackpool had three glorious chances to take the lead and missed them all. The players look nervous and by half time my fingernails have gone. We are 1-0 up courtesy of a Carlton Cole effort only for Ince to take the wind out of our sails. To get our passing game going is a Titanic struggle but it is Blackpool who are sunk. Close to the final whistle Vaz Te pounces to smash home the winner and we are promoted. This is one day when I can agree with big Sam, it's only the result that counts. The team had just made us so happy by gaining promotion yet in the car on the way back home we are already discussing who has to go and who needs to be brought in. It's definitely the most exciting way to go up, but it sure is hard work on the 'old ticker'.

# Last of the Summer Wine

Now the hard work begins and we must get our new signings right. Eleven million pounds for Matt Jarvis? If that wasn't bad enough then they must have seen us coming when Modibo Maiga was purchased. Who is recommending these players to us and what medication is he taking. A club record is broken in order for us to pay £15 million pounds for Andy Carroll. When fully fit I consider him to be an asset and a real handful for any defence. On the down side he appears to be injury prone. He is the only player I know to get injured on A Question of Sport.  Let's hope he can get the goals to keep us in this division as this season is all about consolidation. We will be up against Queens Park Rangers and the chance to renew the rivalry between me and Mike beckons. The first meeting between us is at their place early in the season and we win 2-1. Now I'm happy to meet up with Mike any time he is ready. He is very knowledgeable about the game, and in the 'banter stakes' can more than hold his own. I remind him of the time when I went to Queens Park Rangers and had trouble with my seat, it faced the pitch. Rangers would end the season rock bottom with just four wins to their credit. Christmas is fast approaching and for Mike I think I might get a QPR sledge (goes downhill really fast). On second thoughts perhaps not as this man has suffered enough.

The lads get me a ticket for another one of the West Ham nights and this one is going to be held at the Cliffs Pavilion in Westcliff. As usual Tony Gale is to host the proceedings. Joining him on the bill are Julian Dicks, Ray Stewart and Geoff Hurst, our three most prolific penalty takers on the same bill. Gale will use all his expertise to coax stories from all three and also relates events to embarrass them as well. During the interval there is an auction of hammers memorabilia, signed pictures and shirts etc. The items attracting the bids are the ones from the seventies and eighties. Nobody seems interested in purchasing anything from the present squad.

A value for money evening ends and our contented trio make our way back to the station. En route we choose to stop and buy some chips and having made our purchase we step outside to chat for a moment. A car then drives past and I hear the sound of smashing, and looking down notice yolk running down my trousers and that I've been egged. They managed to miss Dave and Trevor but some of the other bystanders were not so lucky. So with egg running down my trousers I begin to walk away. Trevor says to me "where are you going" and I told him "well I'm not going to hang around and see if he's going for the full English". We get to the station to see the train pulling out. With chips flying everywhere, our Usain Bolt impressions are good enough to see us get on board. What a relief or so we thought, we were laughing and chatting, blissfully unaware that in our haste we had jumped on the wrong train. It wasn't until we thought that we must be getting close to Basildon that we looked out of the window and realised we had gone straight past. The earliest it was going to stop would be Stanford Le Hope. So we get off there only to find it in darkness and all locked up. The three of us scramble around the floor hoping to find a ticket to unlock a barrier in order to get out. This took some time but eventually we are out. Our next move is to walk to the taxi rank and we will have to get a cab home. We wait for what feels like an eternity and still no sign of a cab. Some guy walks past and we ask him if he has seen any cabs about. He then tells us that we won't get a cab from where we are as they stopped using that rank months ago. He told us that we had to walk into the town to get one. Reluctantly we go on a sponsored walk to find the cab office. Typical of our luck the man in charge says that it is a busy night and that we will have a bit of a wait before one is available.  Eventually we get a taxi to Basildon and I get home at around 1.30a.m. As I am getting ready for bed I awake Marie and she remarks "you're late", to which I replied "yeah, a couple of them stuttered when they spoke" and fell into bed after another eventful evening.

On the field we finish in mid table which when looking at the bigger picture is not too bad. In nineteen away games we only manage to find the back of the net eleven times which does not make for pleasant reading. This is even less than the three teams who get relegated. Should I just be grateful that we will still be here next season? I want the cake and the cherry on the top, to win and play entertaining football. Only now it is a harsh reality that failure constitutes a financial disaster so I should cut Sam some slack. It's a lot easier to accept his ideas when watching on the box than parting with my hard earned cash to witness this in person.

We are making up for lost time on the socialising front and when the lad's call round Martin says that it's just like the Last of the Summer Wine. With this in mind I am quick to inform him that he can be replaced or a rent increase could be implemented! How do you measure success in 2013-14? Of our last eleven games we suffer eight defeats but live to fight another day in this division. Straws and clutching are the two words that readily spring to mind. A good run in the league cup pairs us with Manchester City in the semi-final. Over the two legs they are fortunate enough to get nine breakaway goals against the run of play to just edge us out. Allardyce fields a weakened side away to Nottingham Forest in the F.A. cup and a 5-0 reversal sums up another sorry day. I'm still of the opinion that a strong line up was the order of the day and that's not me just speaking in hindsight. A decent run in the cup would have been most welcome, we were huge underdogs to beat Manchester City but a strong team against Nottingham Forest would have been expected to win and then who knows what may have happened. Over the course of the season we can still only manage to average one goal per game. Great credit must go to the team for beating spurs three times in a season, that's how to get the fans back on side.

These West Ham talk nights are proving such a hit with the fans that the Cliffs Pavilion organise another evening. We have certainly got the bug and this time there will be ten of us going including Steve Lloyd. Steve himself has been having health problems of his own and it is good to see him out enjoying himself and looking well, I wish him all the best and truly mean it. Back to the night out and this one should be the best one so far. Due to appear are Billy Bonds, Alan Devonshire, David Cross, Geoff Pike, Billy Jennings, Keith Robson and Alan Taylor. They don't disappoint and we have a great evening as they talk us through their time at Upton Park. In their day they were never paid the mega bucks that today's players are in receipt of. It goes without saying that they were paid more than Joe Public got but the gulf was never as wide as it is today. Leading on from that we learn that they are all still in employment. Alan Taylor for a funeral director, Keith Robson at an airport, Billy Jennings is a football agent, David cross is a scout for Oldham Athletic and Geoff Pike works for the F.A. The entire evening was funny and informative and we had a stress free journey home for a change.

# **Injury Time**

I am more optimistic looking forward to the coming season than I have been for quite a while. Aaron Cresswell, Cheikho Kouyate, Alex Song and Diafra Sakho improve the quality of the squad. For some unknown reason we no longer appear to have any youngsters able to make the step up from the academy. Over the past few years many get the odd game here and there but none can claim a decent run in the side, the latest one being Danny Potts. In the modern game the turnover of players each season seems to be on the increase. So many foreign players arrive and one minute they are kissing the badge and the next minute planning their own transfer. Mark Noble has a well deserved testimonial on the horizon and loyal players such as he will be a thing of the past. Maybe they are being badly advised by agents who want to move players on for financial gain. When players have a get out clause written in to their contract allowing them to leave if another club triggers that fee, how does any other club know what that figure is unless the agent has made it known?

Over the years we have wasted more than enough money on players who were never worth their fee and never produced any sort of form. I could fill a page or two listing them but I am not going to as any true hammers fan will have little difficulty in remembering them.

Steve Lloyd has reached his 60th birthday and is having a party to celebrate this millstone (sorry milestone) occasion. I am guilty of not being in contact with Steve as often as I should have and therefore more than delighted to get an invitation and it's my pleasure to gratefully accept. Dave, Brenda and Trevor will be attending also. It was good to see so many faces from our footballing past, not only old team mates but some who we played against. An unexpected bonus was seeing some of my old team mates from Basildon B.C. Steve has a lovely family and even though I had not spoken to his wife Viv for some time she was as friendly and bubbly as ever.

Here I am celebrating his 60th birthday and it seems like only yesterday as I remember that first meeting as ten year olds. I offer to get the first round in and I think it was two lucazades, two sanatogens, one horlicks and one night nurse (how times have changed). It would be a double celebration for us that evening as it was Marie's birthday. I am not about to reveal her age here as I would quite like to carry on breathing. We had a great evening as we always do when in the company of these lads and their better halves.

Having previously recounted my own health problems and Steve dealing with his own issues it's now Dave and Trevor's turn to get acquainted with their doctors. Dave has to have both hips replaced (ouch), and Trevor has a bad back. I tell him that's nothing, Arsenal have four. Trevor's back problem is serious; in the morning when the alarm rings he can't get off it. All joking aside he is in a lot of discomfort and could open his own chemist with the amount of medication he needs. He works in a physical job which can't help, but carries on regardless. But he still has to be careful when lifting his wallet.

In desperate need of a pick me up we book a weekend break. This getting old lark isn't all it's cracked up to be. Accompanied by Dave and Brenda we are off to Potters Leisure resort and it is just what the doctor ordered, it's nice to have something good happen once in a while.

Back at Upton Park we are in fourth position at Christmas. It's a well known fact that other fans love to trot out that old saying that West Ham come down with the Christmas decorations. So of course we provide them with the perfect ammunition to have a go by only winning two of our last seventeen games. Allardyce has kept us up again but I still can't seem to warm to him, and it looks like I'm not the only one. This is the end of the road for Sam and I think it will be good for all concerned. He needs a new challenge and we need to get our identity back. I had the impression that a lot of times we were not going out there to win, merely to contain.

My birthday arrives and now I am 60. These days I am so easy to buy for as West Ham related pressy's are never refused. West Ham monopoly, shirts, books and D.V.D.'s all come my way. Well what can you give the man who has got everything (penicillin?). As you should be well aware of by now, and if not then you haven't been paying attention that I am a fan of the West Ham talk nights. Out on D.V.D. is the boys of 86 dinner. This is like having one of those nights in your own front room. The squad are interviewed by Tony Gale (he gets everywhere) with T.V. footage shown in between. I invite the lads round to watch this, and who says nostalgia isn't what it used to be. We talk about our times of following the irons and the time fly's past, and I always feel better after an evening in their company. During the evening Marie brought in refreshments so I paused the D.V.D. We then went on a walk down memory lane indulging in a session of that age old pastime of 'do you remember when'? Dave and Trevor tell the story of a game away at Southampton (I wasn't present at this one but I'm sure I must have had a note from my mum excusing me). This was in the days before trains had the automatic sliding doors of today. To get out of the carriage you had to turn the handle on the on the door which would then open outwards. The boys had taken a Watneys party 7 with them. For those of you too young to remember this was an extra large can that held seven pints of beer. Anyway on arrival at Southampton Trevor gets off first and swings the door shut behind him. Right behind him Dave was getting off but taking a swig from the party 7 can. The carriage door swung back with such force that it rammed the can right back into Dave's face. It did this with such force it left a very large red ring round the outside of Dave's face.  Dave got plenty of admiring glances throughout the day as this would take some considerable time to fade. Luckily for Trevor, Dave eventually saw the funny side and allowed him to live.

I can fondly recall my dad telling me about his favourite games players etc. and now I find I am doing the exact same thing with my children. I find myself telling them of our trip to the Abbey Stadium when we were away to Cambridge United. We had parked up some way from the ground and asked for directions to the stadium. We asked some random guy who told us "just follow the crowd". We did this and ended up in Tesco's.

Melissa and Martin have grown up with Sky sports and more recently B.T. sports dominating the fixture schedule with their 'Martini policy' (anytime, anyplace, anywhere). I explain to them of the time back in the early seventies when this was such a rare occurrence. The country was in the grip of industrial unrest and power restrictions were implemented. A three day working week was enforced and I was knackered as this was two days more than I was used to. We were playing Hereford United at home in the F.A. cup on a Monday with a 2.15.pm kick off. Various parts of the country had different working days, and I was lucky enough that this was not one of mine and was free to attend. I never anticipated a full house and was fortunate to get in just before they shut the gates. A hat-trick from Geoff Hurst saw us 3-1 winners on a day when the atmosphere seemed so surreal.

# **Mixed Emotions**

The king is dead so long live the king. So Sam Allardyce departs having been rated by me as an adequate stop gap. Even up to the day he left he wanted us to embrace his tactics and style of play, while still refusing to understand or ignore what was the West Ham way. The media constantly warn us to be careful what we wish for as with the move to the large Olympic Stadium at Stratford on the horizon relegation is not an option. Surely there is always a certain amount of risk when changing a manager at any time. He had steadied the ship but I could never see him doing much better.

Slaven Bilic takes over the reins and his record seems to stack up having had a good spell at Besiktas in Turkey and managing the Croatian national side. Being an ex-hammer should also help in getting us supporters on side. With Dimitri Payet, Michail Antonio, Manuel Lanzini arriving this means that we have now added pace and flair to our side, the type of signings to excite the fans. Other good signings are Darren Randolph, Pedro Obiang and Sam Byram are all players who could do well for us. This is a season that will live long in the memory. A bitter sweet season because this was the best football I have seen us play for some while, but sad because this is to be the last ever at Upton Park. Alright so we didn't win anything, but what was served up before us on the pitch did most definitely sweeten the pill. Concerning the move is another case of mixed emotions for me. Financial needs dictate that we need to go but I am not sure I want us to leave our unique home. After all, having us fans so close to the pitch has helped us to win many a battle in the past.

Steve lets us know that his local pub is having a Julian Dicks night and do I want a ticket (does the pope shit in the woods?) It will be along the lines of the type of nights previously attended by us, only this one will be of a more intimate nature. Numbers are restricted and tickets are at a premium, no worries for us though as once again Steve delivers the goods and we are in. When I first saw Julian in a speaking role he seemed a little nervous and not that comfortable. In this atmosphere he was brilliant. He spoke honestly, was funny and not once did he try to evade a question in the Q and A section. He has a genuine affection for the fans and the standing ovation he received was richly merited. He gave his time generously, posing for photos and signing autographs.

Talking about the demise of Upton Park was high on the agenda that evening. We all agreed that having spent so much of our lives there we have to go one last time to pay our respects. The place has meant so much to us and played a huge part in all our lives we owe it to ourselves to get together and make this happen. The person who did make it happen was Steve. Our 'social secretary' and go to guy in these situations never lets us down. He comes up with the goods and one last trip to the Holy Land has been arranged for the F.A. cup tie with Wolverhampton Wanderers.

There will be ten of us going to this one and as usual I am looking forward to being in their company.

Trevor had our tickets and the plan was to all meet up at Basildon railway station. Dave made the decision to go to Laindon station as this would be more convenient for him, and when our train arrived we would make ourselves known and he would join up with us. However, two factors came into play that we did not plan for that were to throw our afternoon into chaos. Firstly, Dave had left home without his mobile phone, and secondly no trains from Basildon would be going to Laindon. This disruption to our plans meant our alternative route was to board a train travelling in the opposite direction and then change. This took us on to a different line involving a longer 'round he houses journey'. Now Trevor has Dave's match ticket and we have no way of letting him know our train will not be coming his way. Trevor had phoned Brenda at home and that is how we found out Dave never had his phone on him, and continued to call at various times throughout the day to see if he had phoned home and she could pass on a message in order to arrange a meet.

We waited around at Barking station for any sign of him with no luck. Our next move was to go out into Barking high street and check out a couple of the pubs we hoped he may have gone into, alas no joy there either. We search around at Upton Park station and checked the pubs in Green Street only to be met with more failure. One last throw of the dice was to check the ticket office, perhaps he may be waiting outside there. We had struck out again and now it's five to three. Dave has never even seen our tickets so would not know which part of the ground we would be entering by. We check a few entrances but the teams are out and we need to get in. We feel bad but what more can we do? Weather wise it is a lousy day. On the pitch we field a pick-and –mix side and we are making heavy weather of disposing our visitors from the lower league, and after all my previous experiences why am I not surprised. The wonderful flowing football I have witnessed from my armchair is not available for me today. Late in the game Carroll and Payet are brought on and we look a bit more like our old selves. Just before the end Jelavic hits a peach of a drive to spare our blushes, but at least we are in the hat for the fourth round draw.

It was fantastic to be present for one last time, but such a shame Dave wasn't with us. Mixed emotions again. We later found out that he had made his own way to the ground and because we all failed to meet up he was forced to buy a ticket from a tout. Our journey home was just as bad. We were soaked to the skin and the trains were still all over the place. More cancellations and a different route home added an extra two hours to my arrival home. Great to see a home win, horrendous journey home; mixed emotions again.

Things are 'bubbling' along quite nicely in the F.A. cup and when the draw is made for the quarter finals we are given an away trip to Manchester United. By this time Melissa has been in a steady relationship for a while and has now moved in with her partner. His name is Dave and he loves West Ham. How does the saying go, the apple never falls far from the tree? They invite

Marie, Martin and me over for Sunday lunch and to watch the cup game on their new 46-inch television. We are playing some good stuff, taking the game to them and I am confident (if you can ever be confident watching West Ham). In the second half Payet delights us with one of his trademark free kicks and I am rehearsing my speech for when I meet up with my Manchester United 'friends'. This has been a season where many crucial decisions have gone against us, and yet another was looming on the horizon. There wasn't too long left when a ball is flashed across the face of our goal. Keeper Darren Randolph comes to collect it but is 'ambushed' en route and they score. A diabolical decision means we come away with a draw. Before the game if offered a draw I would have taken it. After the game I feel robbed we should have won. Mixed emotions again. At least we got to have a lovely day with Melissa and Dave.

Where the F.A. cup is concerned I am not ashamed to admit that I am an old fashioned traditionalist. I loved the fact that the draw was made on Monday lunchtime. Either at school or at work there would always be someone who had a radio for us all to gather round and eagerly listen to. There were no penalty shoot-outs and games were played until there was a winner. Most years this would invariably throw up one tie that went to three replays before a winner emerged. It was just the final that was played at Wembley so if you got there it was magical. Nowadays with the semi-finals being held there, for me some of the gloss disappears from the achievement of getting to the final. For all the above reasons the F.A. cup was special to me and now finance dictated that changes had to be made and I find that sad.

When out shopping in Basildon I bump into Phil Parmenter, since he moved to Surrey our paths have hardly crossed. During our chat he informs me that he is looking to get a place to live back in Basildon which I am glad to hear. Perhaps we can rekindle our friendship, I am thinking to myself. He then continues to say that the main reason for the move is that he and Debbie have split up and are going their separate ways. Mixed emotions again. It's been too long since I last spoke to Ian so Melissa takes advantage of social media to track him down for me. I waste no time in calling him having been furnished with his new telephone number to find out how he and his wife Elaine are doing. We have spoken a few times since and agree we should try to meet up.

The Julian Dicks night at the local pub was such a hit they organise another one with the latest guests being Phil Parkes and Ray Stewart. Steve, Dave, Trevor and I are quick to get our names down for a ticket. There was to be a slight variation in the way this one was to be conducted. No host would be guiding them into topics of conversation the entire evening was to be questions from the floor. Once again with limited numbers anyone who wanted to speak had a chance. Food had been provided so there was a mid-evening break. Whilst getting the food I was standing beside Phil Parkes and we chatted one to one for around ten minutes. He was very pleasant to talk to and seemed interested in what I had to say (either that or he does great impressions). He even asked me a couple of questions for my views on West Ham related subjects. Both Phil and Ray spent a considerable amount of time with the fans. Long after the event had officially ended they were still there posing with fans and signing merchandise that was put before them. Ray loves being classed as a 'jockney' and both he and Phil gave value for money with their wit and insight into all things West Ham United. We left at 11.15 with the pair of them still surrounded by excited fans.

The team have given us a season to cherish as we bid farewell to Upton Park. We had played with style, passion and no little skill. We should have finished higher in the league and would have done so had it not been for some awful decisions that went against us. I'm thinking of Lanzini's goal wrongly disallowed against Arsenal. Penalties awarded against us that never were against Chelsea and Leicester. Kouyate should not have been sent off against Crystal Palace, all of which would rob us of eight more points and Champions league may well have been on the cards. Such is life. It's been great but could have been better, mixed emotions again.

Sadness enters our lives when Dave calls to let me know that Steve's mum Doreen has sadly passed away. It goes without saying we shall be attending the funeral as that is what you do for a mate; you want to be there for them. It was good that we would all be together again but a shame it had to be under these circumstances. Mixed emotions again. I'm now seeing more of Queens Park Rangers Mike as he now works in Ladbrokes where I go to place my bets. Not that he ever was a stranger. For over fifteen years he ran a Fantasy football league and me and Martin would regularly enter teams. There would generally be around about eighty of us taking part and on a weekly basis Mike would come round with the up-dated league tables and we would chew the fat with regards to our footballing favourites.

We go back to the late sixties in the days of the Big Match with Brian Moore on a Sunday afternoon. As a group of young lads we would all watch the programme and as soon as it was over we would all gather on the school football pitch for a game and re-enact what we had just seen. Some of our afternoon games would have as many as fifteen a side.

Over many years of watching the irons I've seen us waste huge amounts of money on terrible signings, bring some in who were adequate and a fair few who performed alright but should have produced the goods on a more consistent basis. But when it comes to idols and legends there has been no shortage. I will pass on selecting an all time favourite eleven but those who would walk straight into my greatest ever squad would be as follows: Parkes, Miklosko, Stewart, Martin, Moore, Dicks, Bonds, Peters, Di Canio, Brooking, Devonshire, Byrne, Hurst, Cottee, Mcavennie, Bryan Robson, Benayoun and Parker.

With special reference to Billy Bonds and Julian Dicks I felt they never got the credit from the media that they deserved. Regarded as 'hard men', but there was so much more to their game than that. Bonds would perform brilliantly at right back, centre back or in mid- field. I can remember going to a Friday night home game against Coventry and Bonds was playing in a forward role and scored twice in a thrilling 5-2 victory. Another stand out moment was his hat-trick from mid-field against Chelsea when we turned them over 3-0.

In the case of Julian, he wasn't the biggest of men but was good in the air. He possessed a 'magic wand' of a left foot and sprayed many superb cross field passes for our forwards. It was a complete miss carriage of justice that neither Bonds nor Dicks were to be rewarded with an England cap. Julian could hit a thirty yard pass and land it on a sixpence (currency, after the groat but before the 50p). It must have been especially frustrating in Julian's case as players were being picked to play for England who were not fit enough to lace his drinks (sorry, that should have read boots). At the time there was some silly rumour doing the rounds that he would get an England call up if he got a proper hairstyle, try telling that to today's players. My favourite goal scored by Julian Dicks came in a 5-3 home win over Oxford United. It was a thunderbolt from around thirty yards. The keeper did well to get out of the way of it as it would have seriously hurt him had it hit him. Both Bonds and Dicks were guilty of the odd transgression but they played with pride and passion. I was watching players who were as desperate for my team to win as I was. They cared about the club the fans and the performance, and I appreciated the fact that they never stopped trying.

I have liked many other players but consider they lacked that extra something to join the list of afore mentioned names. So for now I will refrain from rolling out another list of 'near misses'.

We are now open for business at Stratford and Melissa suggests we should go, and with that in mind books two seats for the Hull City fixture. With so many conflicting reports going about with regards to the new set up we want to see for ourselves and form our own opinions. Also this would be an ideal opportunity to get in touch with Ian and see if he wants to meet up. Thankfully he says yes and another plan is lifted from the drawing board. Melissa and I get a train from Basildon directly to Stratford, a good start. We then experience quite a walk to the stadium which I find soul-less compared to the 'Green Street meander'. Previously in this book I have described how the time spent outside the stadium and the walk to the ground became an integral part of our day. This one proves to be oh so different. No sign of the stalls that we loved to patronise. There is a lack of atmosphere with the missing 'watering holes' and pie and mash shops. New match day rituals will have to be sought out. I was never one hundred per cent against the prospect of having to move home but I would have been more willing to buy into the project had we been going to a stadium that had been built and designed with us in mind. This stadium however large it may be was clearly never designed for football. Making the pitch larger to bring it closer to the fans has not worked out either. Melissa calls Ian to find out of his whereabouts and we finally get to meet. We met up inside the ground and what a pleasure to see him again. A warm handshake for me and a kiss for Melissa (so glad he got it that way round), leads Ian to ask about the lads and their well-being. We speak of happy days in times past with great affection, but only for a brief time as kick off is approaching. He appears well and the famous five should really all get together again. This meeting was as much a part of the day as the match itself. Ian still retains his status as a season ticket holder and is seated near the half way line, and assures me the view is very good. Friends of mine who have been before had warned me to take binoculars with me. I am seated further away from the action than I had hoped, but it wasn't as bad as I had feared. Ian has a very good view and mine is 'okayish', so there you have it football has and always will be about opinions.

A more pleasing sight was to see Clyde Best give a pitch side interview during the half time break. The main facts of the game are Hull hit the woodwork three times and we hit the back of the net once. I feel this larger pitch has an adverse effect on our play, and so it is left for Mark Noble to secure the three points for us from the penalty spot.

Getting to Upton Park station with 35,000 people leaving was hard enough; now with close to 60,000 fans making their way out surely this was going to be a mission. As I sit behind the goal looking around the stadium my mind takes me back to that magical day in 1962 when as a young boy I made my first visit to Upton Park. Back then I stood there in amazement and bewilderment at how great this place was. Today is different I am now sitting here thinking I'm not too sure about this. Change in any form of life is always problematic at the start. Given time perhaps I will accustom to the new surroundings and embrace the change, only time will tell. With the development of new match day rituals and good performances on the pitch this will hopefully make settling in an easier proposition. Deep down I always knew the first visit would be the most difficult.

An overview of my day, I have now been to the new stadium, I have seen us pick up three points, I have met up with Ian, and I have seen Clyde Best. But the undoubted highlight was that Melissa still wants to spend time with her dad and go to the game. Marie may well think that football and West Ham dominate my life but I would have to disagree, after all I have been with her for thirty seven seasons. I have never once regretted being a West Ham fan even though success has been somewhat fleeting, but I never signed up for that anyway. We certainly have the best fans. Admittedly some players do get stick but the fans will forgive anyone having a bad game, but what they will not forgive is a distinct lack of effort. We most definitely have the best 'scribes'. Pete May, Robert Banks, Brian Belton Martin Godleman and Brian Williams each one so talented. West Ham have always been my team, to praise or to criticise but desert, never.

I was rather hoping that Dimitri Payet would make it impossible for me to leave him out of my all-time great's squad. The club bent over backwards to accommodate him via wage increases, a loyalty bonus and a long term contract. I always think it a shame when a player I really rate chooses to leave. But I also believe that there is a right way and a wrong way to go about it. When it becomes apparent that this season sleeves had to be rolled up in preparation for a battle he didn't have the stomach to fight for us.

He just thought that to 'down tools' was the correct way forward for him. In my book I considered that to be bang out of order. The club were paying him excellent money he was entitled to go out and perform to the best of his ability until a deal was confirmed. So in effect having a player on a long term contract means nothing if he has the power to refuse to play in order to engineer the move of his choice. He held a gun to our heads knowing if we kept him at the club possibly training with the kids his value would be decreasing all the while. That may even cause an adverse effect on the youngsters if he is promoting that type of attitude to them. If what I read was to be believed that he was upsetting various first team players then he had to go. Getting the best possible price for him now was the only way out. In the past other players have wanted to leave but still put the shirt on and gave of their best. They never held the club to ransom so why should he be allowed to be different. When seeking a move I think it is in the player's interest as well as the clubs that he should go out and perform.  By playing well he may attract the attention of a whole host of clubs, while at the same time this would provide an insight into his character and temperament. The whole sorry saga left a nasty taste in the mouth, from hero to zero how the mighty have fallen, and I hope he feels distraught at not being included in my squad!

Over the years we all get to hear stories about the beautiful game and I could not complete this book without inflicting one of my favourites upon you. It concerns Paul Gascoigne and the time he went back to St. James Park to watch Newcastle United play. He was driving away after the game and got stopped at a set of traffic lights. Looking in his rear view mirror he noticed a Newcastle fan running after him. He tapped on gazza's window and when he opened it this fan proceeded to go off on one. "We idolised you gazza, you were a legend to us and you betrayed us and went to play for those southern bastards spurs, we hate you gazza, hate you".

The lights changed and gazza closed the window and drove off. A few hundred yards down the road gazza gets stopped at another set of traffic lights. He looks in the rear view mirror and is once again confronted with the sight of the same fan still chasing him. He reaches gazza's car and once again taps on the window. As soon as it is opened he carries on with his abusive tirade.

"And another thing gazza, the whole country loved you when you played for England and you sold out and left our country to go and play in Italy. We worshipped you. You mercenary, money grabbing, greedy bastard, we hate you gazza, hate you". And so the lights change and he drives away.

A couple of hundred yards down the road the traffic lights halt gazza's progress once more. A glance into the rear view mirror confirms his worst fear as the disgruntled fan is still chasing him. Now completely fed up gazza thinks I'm not having any more of this and drops his trousers and sticks his arse out of the window. When the fan gets near to the window he takes one look and says "AND AS FOR YOU BEARDSLEY".

A night out is planned and Marie and I go out to dinner with Dave, Brenda, Trevor, Melissa and Dave. This evening will give me the ideal opportunity to run past them some of the anecdotes that I may include in this book. It will also allow me to check with them that I have the details correct. Some stories make it in and some do not, but it leads us all to have a good time re-living the days of our miss spent youth.

# Extra Time

On reading this page I do hope that you have managed to stay with me on my journey, and are not just randomly flicking through the pages. If that is the case then I would like to say a big thank you and if you have enjoyed it half as much as I have, then I enjoyed it twice as much as you did. An update on a more personal level leads me to inform you that I am due to return to Addenbrooks hospital where the prospect of another operation is awaiting in my battle to combat Meneires disease.

As they say time waits for no man, and now we are all past our 63rd birthdays but still keep in touch. The odd competition win still comes my way and it wasn't too long ago that I won a party night out for ten of us. The collecting of 'special' programmes continues and one day may be worth something, the last one at Upton Park and the first at the London stadium should reap some reward as I plan to pass them all on to Melissa and Martin.

I have been fortunate to have seen some great individual players down the years, but for me the best team has to be the side of the early eighties. Winning the F.A. cup galloping away with the division two title and breaking records along the way, runners up in the league cup final and playing the brand of football associated with our club. The lads of 1986 achieved our highest ever position of third place and came so close to claiming the championship itself. They too played with style but I'm afraid I have to rate them a close second. Not being able to push on from that great season was probably John Lyalls downfall. He should have strengthened the squad while we were on top. The signings of McKnight and Kelly were uninspiring and a huge disappointment and did him no favours. Having said that I felt he was deserving of another position 'upstairs' to retain his services in some capacity.

I had an extremely happy home life, and the best upbringing that I could have hoped for. Through my love of West Ham United I have made many special friends and they will always remain so. Somehow along the way I managed to convince Marie to marry me (my best ever signing), and I could not wish for a better wife or mother for my children. I am so proud of Melissa and Martin, not just because they walk the claret and blue path but for the type of person that they have grown to become. It's been a joy to have them in my life and they most certainly have brightened my life (they never switch a light off). I do hope life smiles upon them as they deserve to be happy. My good luck allowed me to see my team win cup finals at Wembley and play in European finals. But do I think I will ever get to see them win the premiership I very much doubt it, but then again I'm forever blowing bubbles....................

Printed in Great Britain
by Amazon